Cats on the Job

Also by Lisa Rogak

Angry Optimist: The Life and Times of Jon Stewart

One Big Happy Family: Heartwarming Stories of Animals Caring for One Another

Dan Brown: The Unauthorized Biography

Dogs of Courage: The Heroism and Heart of Working Dogs Around the World

The Dogs of War: The Courage, Love, and Loyalty of Military Working Dogs

And Nothing But the Truthiness: The Rise (and Further Rise) of Stephen Colbert

Michelle Obama in Her Own Words: The Views and Values of America's First Lady

Barack Obama in His Own Words

Haunted Heart: The Life and Times of Stephen King

A Boy Named Shel: The Life and Times of Shel Silverstein

Cats on the Job

50 Fabulous Felines Who Purr, Mouse,
and Even Sing for Their Supper

LISA ROGAK

THOMAS DUNNE BOOKS

ST. MARTIN'S GRIFFIN

NEW YORK

THOMAS DUNNE BOOKS.
An imprint of St. Martin's Press.

CATS ON THE JOB. Copyright © 2015 by Lisa Rogak. All rights reserved. Printed in China.
For information, address St. Martin's Press, 175 Fifth Avenue, New York, N.Y. 10010.

"Miao" by Dilys Laing reproduced courtesy of David Laing.

www.thomasdunnebooks.com
www.stmartins.com

Designed by Omar Chapa

The Library of Congress Cataloging-in-Publication Data is available upon request.

ISBN 978-1-250-07237-5 (trade paperback)
ISBN 978-1-4668-8399-4 (e-book)

St. Martin's Griffin books may be purchased for educational, business, or promotional use. For information on bulk purchases, please contact the Macmillan Corporate and Premium Sales Department at
1-800-221-7945, extension 5422, or write to specialmarkets@macmillan.com.

First Edition: October 2015

10 9 8 7 6 5 4 3 2 1

For Bob DiPrete and Poochie, aka Reagan

Contents

Cats on the Job

Introduction

While some naysayers may believe that the only job that a cat is capable of performing is locating and then occupying the warmest spot in the house for hours on end, there are countless hardworking cats around the world that prove otherwise. In recent years, dogs have received attention for doing everything from sniffing out cancer in test tubes to participating in the raid on Osama bin Laden, but cats have not been just idly standing by. Indeed, felines of all stripes are earning their keep today in a surprising variety of jobs.

Even many cat lovers think that the best job for a cat would be CMO, or Chief Mousing Officer. But while many cats are initially hired for this particular skill — and they do excel in that field — the truth is that once a cat moves into a mouse-infested barn or warehouse and demonstrates to the local rodent population who's in charge, it's a brave, brave mouse that dares to venture back onto the premises. After all, the lingering scent of *eau de feline* is usually enough to discourage even the most famished mouse from taking his chances.

Once a cat's mouse-catching responsibilities drop to maintenance levels — in some cases, this occurs within a day or two of starting work — many felines make a career change and become full-time sleep researchers. However, for others, it's the exact moment when they seize control of their destiny and begin to pursue their true occupational path.

Of course, some cats are just not good at mousing. These so-called slackers may actually be the Steve Jobs of felines, so intent on doing their true jobs that they thoroughly ignore anything as normal as rodents. As you'll discover in *Cats on the Job,* these career-focused felines can be found working as a gregarious hotel concierge, a bike messenger's loyal assistant, or a bookstore's director of public relations and marketing. Some even provide therapy and comfort as service cats: one helps an autistic boy learn how to make his way in the world, while another lends a paw to a girl to help manage her diabetes.

It's an idea that is catching on. A group in Los Angeles called Working Cats has been placing felines at businesses around the city, primarily for rat patrol, while a similar organization in San Francisco called Cats on the Job contracts a number of SPCA shelter cats out to a local arts organization where they serve as guides as well as security detail.

On the whole, working cats are not particularly picky about their salary. Although some of the felines profiled in *Cats on the Job* have signed employment contracts specifying that they receive their salary in the form of cat food or fresh fish, the pay is usually not a huge concern to the average cat employee; while they're unlikely to ever unionize, some do strike over poor working conditions.

A century ago, a British government worker named Stella Alleyne marveled at the actions of a particular cat who had successfully presided over the cafeteria at the Ministry of Agriculture for a number of years. The cat clearly loved his job and the people he worked with. One day, an employee from the nearby Fisheries Department decided to borrow him to help out with a mouse problem in their building and simply took him without asking. At first, the cat didn't fight back or yowl in protest. But when he arrived at the new building the employees were bitterly disappointed when the cat did nothing but sit and watch as the mice scampered by.

"As this was not his department, he simply refused to take action," said Alleyne. In a few days, he was back at the Ministry of Agriculture, happily pursuing and catching any mice that happened to cross his path.

Of course, some bosses may just fire a recalcitrant employee—whether two- or four-legged—but people who happen to work alongside a cat view this pickiness as a mere by-product of having a feline coworker.

"I have seen cats working in warehouses who are toasted by the men who work with them, in glasses brimming with moonlight," wrote author Oswell Blakeston in *Working Cats*, his 1963 book-length ode to gainfully employed felines. "A working cat appreciates a good billet [living quarters], but most of all he takes into consideration the comradeship he will receive if he puts a paw-mark to a contract for his services."

It's impossible to force a cat to do anything; an old saying is that you have to make the cat think it's his own idea, whereas a dog is typically so eager to please that he'll do your bidding regardless of the task. Simply put, cats are more discriminating about where they choose to spend their energies.

But when they do discover a vocation they like, they'll happily spend all their waking hours at it—and their napping ones, too. Fortunately, this book is filled with fifty different examples of cats who, as Blakeston put it, "have chosen to give their life a mission by fulfilling certain specialized duties."

Which is pretty good advice for humans as well.

Crossing Guard Cat

Some cats are street smart and know the exact moment to cross a busy street to avoid disaster.

But a cat in West Richland, Washington, went one step further: He took a job helping schoolchildren navigate across the road from bus to building.

One day, in the beginning of the 2011 school year, a black cat named Sable showed up at the Enterprise Middle School and watched the crossing guards do their jobs. Monti Franckowiak, safety patrol coordinator at the school, said it didn't take long before Sable pitched in, watching what she did and then mimicking her actions from the other side of the street. "My head is always moving as I keep an eye on everything around me," said Franckowiak. "Sable did the same thing. He'd monitor the students and traffic from his corner, occasionally walk out with the safety patrol as they guided students in the crosswalk, and greet students and community members as they walked by."

The cat showed up like clockwork twice each day, commuting to work from his nearby home, and soon demonstrated such prowess at his job that the school presented him with an official orange safety vest to help him carry out his duties. On days when the crosswalk would become slick, Sable would try to rub up against every student who came by. Franckowiak thought it was the cat's way of telling students to slow down and be careful. On snowy days, Sable still came to work and perched on top of a pile of plowed snow on the corner as he watched over students trudging through the snow.

One bitterly cold December morning, Sable was on the job as usual even though the wind chill was ten degrees. Everything was extra slippery that day and it wasn't long before a boy slipped and fell in the crosswalk. Sable dashed over to him and sniffed his tears and rubbed against his arm. "It's okay, Sable's got this," the boy called out to Franckowiak.

"Sable knew his job was important, and he knew he was keeping those students safe," she said. In fact, many people would drive by slower than the speed limit just so they could get a look at the feline crossing guard.

Safety patrol students regarded Sable as part of the team, and unlike some of his two-legged coworkers, he always showed up on time for his job. As Franckowiak headed out to her post, Sable would already be there pacing at the very edge of the curb as if to say, "Hurry up, let's get to work."

Farmer Cat

When Ken Cook of Dunbarton, New Hampshire, first launched his post-retirement business dabbling in organic vegetables — selling both to consumers at farmers' markets and to local restaurants on a wholesale basis — he knew all along that his feline companion, a buff orange longhaired rescue named Rusty, was going to run the show.

So naturally he named the business Rusty's Heirloom Tomatoes. He also left no doubt who was in charge by placing the cat at the very top of the organizational flowchart, naming him CEO, which is the only way any self-respecting working cat would have it. Cook put himself at the bottom of the totem pole, as grunt and worker bee.

When he started the farm in 2009, Cook fully intended to involve Rusty in all aspects of the work. "We wanted to attract both children and adults to the business and make it fun and educational to learn about the many different kinds of tomatoes," said Cook. "What better way to accomplish that than with a cat?"

Rusty wholeheartedly agreed. In addition to showing up at the farmers' market, customers also visit Rusty's house, which he graciously has allowed Ken and his wife, Greta, to share with him. Sometimes Rusty leads tours of the gardens and the small shed where produce is displayed for sale. Occasionally, the cat becomes so excited about his tomatoes that he'll jump in the trunk of a customer's car so he can see them enjoy the fruits of his labor at home.

Cook also crossbreeds tomatoes, saves

seeds, and conducts trial breeding. He even named a tomato after the cat: Rusty's Oxheart. The multicolored red, green, and pink oxheart is traditionally rare, and Ken felt it reflected Rusty's uniqueness.

Once the business took off, CEO Rusty decided to let his human business partners do a little more of the heavy lifting. Rusty runs the farm from a cozy sunroom off the back of the house where he can peruse seed catalogs and farming magazines and help supervise both planting and harvesting by gazing out at the raised beds that cover almost an acre of the farm.

Bookstore Cat

Books and cats go together, well, like books and cats. Fans of the written word — as well as the folks who pen them — have long been aficionados of cats due to their inclination to sit still for long periods of time and be quiet.

So it's no surprise that of all the working cat-egories in this book, by far the highest number of potential candidates to include are the cats who help run bookstores. It was difficult to pick one to profile, but a cat named Boswell in Shelburne Falls, Massachusetts, finally won the honors. In fact, the store is actually named for its feline employee, though after twenty years in business, there have been five different cats at the bookstore who have gone by that name, ranging from a Maine coon cat to the current resident, a female tuxedo cat.

Nancy Eisenstein, the human owner of Boswell's Books, said that the current Boswell is perfectly suited for the rigors of the job. "She has the ideal personality for a bookstore cat," says Eisenstein. "She's friendly and affectionate without being intrusive and instinctively knows who to greet and who to avoid. She loves children and is infinitely patient with toddlers who want to chase her

around the store."

Boswell's job description requires her to excel at a variety of skills: In addition to greeting customers and looking adorable while she sleeps in the window or recycle bin, she serves as the primary focus of the store's marketing program. It helps that the cat is extremely photogenic: Her image appears on the store's logo, bookmarks, and T-shirts as well as Boswell's pin-up calendar. And a local candy maker has created dark and white chocolate truffles shaped like a cat modeled after her.

Indeed, Boswell is so good at her job that she even attracts people who aren't book lovers. "The first step to being successful in retail is getting people into your store," said Eisenstein. "Even nonreaders will come in to meet her, and often leave with earrings, a puzzle or a game that catches their eye on the way out."

Eisenstein feels she's lucked out with Boswell the Fifth, describing how the decision to hire a shelter cat at a store where many different kinds of people are going in and out can be a real crapshoot. "While they may seem friendly with one person, they may not do well interacting with a large number of people every day," she said. "We were extremely fortunate to hire this particular cat, who thrives on being with the public and has such an easygoing temperament."

Office Cat

The insurance industry is typically a pretty buttoned-up business, with little room for the merriment and/or the chaos that would result from having an independent-minded feline employee in charge.

However, the human staff members at Affirmative Risk Management, an insurance claims company in Little Rock, Arkansas, welcome the unpredictability and then some. Not only do they have two office cats, but they also have a couple of canine employees as well.

London — whose official title is Vice President of Claims — is a calico cat named for the venerable British insurance company Lloyd's of London. Her job duties include shredding paper, hacking up hair balls onto legal documents, and killing birds, mice, snakes, and the occasional squirrel on her lunch hour. She'll then drag her prey over to Chantal Roberts, a human colleague who shares her job title, perhaps in the hopes of getting a raise or promotion.

London's energy level is in sharp contrast to ARM's other feline employee, a white and black cat named Cat — short for Catastrophe. As Vice President of

Administration, Cat is pretty laidback and content to spend most of his time overseeing others' work.

As part of their job duties, Cat and London will sit in on job interviews with potential employees, though Roberts admits she often forgets to tell candidates in advance about her animal colleagues because they're such an ingrained part of the office culture. Once, Roberts interviewed a man for a position where he'd be required to visit people at home, and she explained that he would often encounter dogs, cats, and other pets. Right on cue, Harley—ARM's canine Vice President of Operations and Marketing—nosed his way into the conference room to check the guy out, and the man jumped out of his chair.

"I asked if he was afraid of dogs, and he said he wasn't," said Roberts. But then London decided it was her turn to ask the candidate a few questions, so she jumped onto the table in front of the man. "At that point, the man yelled, 'No! Just, no!' and ran out the door, which set off a chain reaction: London was disappointed she didn't get petted, and Harley thought the man was engaging in a game of chase, so he ran after him."

Another time, independent auditors spent the day at the office to review the firm's work. An auditor was working in a conference room when he suddenly yelled. Roberts and a few staffers ran to see what the commotion was, but only found Cat with his head in the auditor's glass of water, calmly drinking. "The auditor seemed dismayed we even thought it was necessary to ask if he wanted another glass," said Roberts.

Messenger Cat

We all know of cats who prefer to stay indoors, who respond to even the slightest suggestion of leaving the house, let alone getting into a moving car, with a veritable storm of hissing, scratching, and the occasional permanent scar inflicted on the nearest human.

But in Philadelphia, there's a cat who not only loves to hurry out of the house every morning, but who joyfully leaps onto the shoulders of her human, impatiently goading him to get on with the day's work of delivering packages and envelopes to customers. The cat then happily sits atop the man's shoulders while he steers his bike through busy city streets, no less.

Bike courier Rudi Saldia and his able feline assistant—a striped tabby named MJ, short for Mary Jane—cover an average of twenty-five miles on two wheels on their rounds every day. While Saldia stays put on his seat, MJ likes to take in different views and will switch back and forth from one shoulder to the other and occasionally drape herself around his neck.

"MJ enjoys the wind rushing through her fur," said Saldia. "She's so comfortable that she never uses her claws. My shoulders and back are scratch-free."

Both feline and human messengers take their job very seriously, so they rarely notice the shocked reactions of pedestrians, though Saldia says it's hard to ignore when somebody yells, "Oh my God, he has a cat on his shoulder!" The regular customers on his route are used to seeing MJ and usually offer up a cat treat and a few head scratches in exchange for the package. New customers, however, are another story. "They're blown away by the fact she arrived via bicycle," said Saldia.

Whenever a customer or onlooker worries about MJ's safety, Saldia soothes their concern. "I'm very confident that the cat would be better off in an accident than I would be, so I'm not worried about taking her out," he said.

Dog Trainer Cat

Dog trainers typically rely on an arsenal of tools to do their jobs, from treats and clickers to squeaky toys. But one resourceful woman employed a very special orange cat named Cheeto to help her train dogs to work as pet detectives in the important mission of finding lost pets.

Kat Albrecht of Federal Way, Washington, launched the Missing Pet Partnership in 2001 to develop community-based lost pet services, training volunteers and professional pet detectives to search for missing pets, both feline and canine. During training sessions, one special feline was required to serve as the "target cat," to help Albrecht evaluate and train cat-detection dogs to sniff out missing cats. Albrecht already had a target cat named Myron, but one cat was just not enough to meet the demand.

"There's a delicate balance in training a dog to find lost cats, and much of it depends upon having the right cat for the job," said Albrecht. "These cats needed to be trained to crate quietly since the dogs needed to learn to use their nose, not their ears, to find the hidden cat."

Cheeto stood out because he had the ideal mix of traits required of a target cat: he was very gregarious, curious, and fearless. Albrecht added that it helped that Cheeto loved dogs: She had four dogs at home at the time and Cheeto fit right into the pack. The dogs were typically segregated in a room by themselves, but Cheeto would regularly jump over the baby gate divider to spend time with his canine pals.

Cheeto worked once a week, year-round, although he did get most holidays off. When he was working, Cheeto's job was to silently lay inside a soft black mesh Sherpa bag that a volunteer hid in different places, such as a pile of heavy brush, under the deck of a house, or even secured up a tree. Then Cheeto waited for the dog to find him. "Our goal was to teach the dogs that cats hide in various locations, high and low, and that if they used their nose to pinpoint the hiding location of the cat, they would be rewarded," Albrecht explained. That "reward" included both treats and one-on-one time with Cheeto.

Cheeto appeared on a number of TV programs as well as at local pet fairs and was nominated for the PAWS Community Hero Pet Awards in 2012. Sadly, Cheeto passed away in the summer of 2014 due to acute pancreatitis. Though Albrecht greatly misses him, she takes comfort in the hundreds of lost cats found by the dogs that Cheeto helped train.

Roommate Cat

Apartments in Japan—especially in Tokyo—are not known for their spaciousness. And though Japanese culture highly reveres cats, many landlords prohibit renters from keeping a cat on the premises, which means that many cats languish in shelters and are left without a job to do.

Tokyo Cat Guardian is a Japanese rescue group that's addressing both problems by contracting a number of its feline residents out to live as roommates in apartments throughout the city. In other words, rent an apartment and automatically get a cat as roommate! The plan accomplishes two objectives: It helps landlords to rent their apartments faster, and tenants don't have to buy anything special for their new feline roommate, since everything is already included.

Yoko Yamamoto founded Tokyo Cat Guardian in 2010 because she was dismayed at the large numbers of homeless cats throughout the city, and she soon started to brainstorm ways to save them. She thought about the many landlords who prohibit animals on their properties, and the lightbulb went off.

"Our aim is to bring the number of cats put down to zero," she said.

She interviews potential human roommates and helps to facilitate the meeting with the landlord. "We are targeting people who have no experience with keeping cats but who would like to, as well as elderly people who want to live with pets but are hesitant because they are concerned that they won't be able to keep them for a long time," she said.

Once a human tenant is approved, they can move in and the cats can start their jobs, although Yamamoto admits the list of the cat's tasks is pretty short.

"The cat's primary job responsibility is to be happy," she said.

A Tokyo-based real estate company named Livinggold is working with Yamamoto to renovate existing apartments to make them more habitable for the feline roommate, adding elevated catwalks and built-in cat trees and towers.

If the human roommate decides to leave the apartment at the end of the lease, she or he has the option of leaving the feline roommate behind in the apartment or adopting and bringing him along to a new residence, in which case, another cat from Tokyo Cat Guardian moves in to take on the job of roommate.

Firehouse Cat

Many folks are familiar with the concept of a firehouse dog, most often in the form of a Dalmatian. But at a firehouse on the Upper East Side of Manhattan, an orange-and-white cat named Carlow takes his job as firehouse cat very seriously.

In the spring of 2011, the firefighters of Engine 22 Ladder 13 responded to a call in the Bronx and encountered an abandoned car that seemed to be meowing. They found a tiny, dirty kitten stuck in one of the tires, brought him back to the station, cleaned him up, and named him Carlow after a local bar where they liked to hang out.

According to Jessica Mikel, who is married to a firefighter in the company, Carlow jumped into his job from the first day, attacking the station's serious rodent problem paws-first. Once his scent permeated the firehouse, a mouse sighting became a rare thing, resulting in a light workload for the cat, altering his job description. "Today, his primary responsibilities are to scare off neighborhood dogs looking for a treat and to keep the probies — newly hired

firefighters on probation — in line, showing everyone that he is boss," said Mikel.

The cat also spends time posing for the many photos that make up his Instagram account, @carlow_firecat, which Mikel helps him run; some of his most popular photos show him snoozing in unusual places on a fire truck. "Carlow is pretty talented in finding comfort in the most peculiar spots," said Mikel. "He makes a tire look cozy."

Carlow actually isn't the first feline firefighter at the station: A cat named Murray lived at the station for fourteen years before he passed on to that great litter box in the sky in 2005. Afterward, the human staff opted for a dog, but soon decided to adopt another cat when the canine staffer wasn't as friendly with the public as Murray had been. Besides, most dogs are not known for their superb rodent-catching skills.

Carlow is such a valued member of the squad that some firefighters even come into the station to visit him on their days off. He also enjoys an international fanbase because of Instagram. Mikel said that people often ask if the firefighters move him off the trucks when they go on a run because they're worried he'll get hurt, but she alleviates their concerns. "Carlow is a very smart kitty," she said. "Before every run, loud tones go off indicating to the guys that it's time to gear up. Carlow knows that these tones mean it's time for him to move to the back of the house, where he holds down the fort until the guys return."

Service Cat

While many cats expect to be waited on hand and foot — and their humans happily indulge them — an increasing number of felines are instead returning the favor: They're choosing to work to help make the life of a physically or emotionally disabled person just a little bit easier. And a Birman cat in Great Britain named Jessi-Cat certainly has achieved that in spades.

Lorcan Dillon was born in 2004, and his parents realized early on that something was wrong. Though he chattered away and communicated readily at home to his parents and brother, in public it was a different story. Upon meeting a stranger, he'd clam up and run and hide, to a much greater degree than other children his age. Eventually he was diagnosed with autism and selective mutism, which left him incapable of communicating with strangers or displaying emotion to anyone, even his parents. He lived a very lonely life at school and at home without friends.

When Lorcan turned six, the family cat died and his mom, Jayne Dillon, brought home a Birman kitten to fill the void. She also secretly dreamed that perhaps another cat might help him to communicate. Happily, Jessi-Cat launched into her job of serving Lorcan almost immediately, and it was clear from the very beginning that they shared a special bond. "I know cats are meant to have a sixth sense, but it is as if this cat understood from day one that Lorcan was vulnerable," said Jayne. "Jessi-Cat has an extraordinary sense of duty and seemed to understand that her role was to stay by Lorcan's side."

About a year after Jessi-Cat arrived at the Dillon household, an incredible thing happened: Lorcan started speaking to the cat and also began to express emotion. Jayne heard her son say "I love you" for the first time in his life. She was so overjoyed to hear him utter those words that she didn't much care that he said them to a cat instead of to her.

From that point on, the little boy progressed rapidly. He started speaking to others in his class, a few words at first, as well as to his teacher. In time, he even read a few sentences aloud in class and started to make friends.

The transformation was so dramatic that Jayne decided to enter Jessi-Cat in the Cats Protection National Cat of the Year Award, an annual program run by a British charity to honor extraordinary cats throughout England.

When Jessi-Cat was nominated, the family was ecstatic and was determined to attend the ceremony. They did, and when Jessi-Cat was announced as Cat of the Year, Lorcan himself headed up to the stage to accept the award. "Lorcan was so proud of Jessi-Cat that he stepped up to the podium to take the award with no hint of nerves," said Jayne. "When we got home, he hugged Jessi-Cat and told her she had won. To me, hearing him talk was like winning all over again."

Boat Captain Cat

As a rule, cats and water don't usually mix. However, there are always exceptions and a cat who lives on a boat and helps to run the ship definitely fits that bill.

Captain Christopher Perunko has lived on a catamaran with his Ragdoll cat, Sunny, in North Key Largo, Florida, since 2010. He works with local scuba-diving charters and contracts out for occasional boat repairs. Captain Chris readily admits that Catptain Sunny's lack of opposable thumbs isn't much help when it comes to these jobs, but that Sunny's position as fellow captain involves a lot of responsibility for the intrepid feline, albeit mostly in a supervisory position.

"Sunny has an insatiable curiosity and a desire to be right in the middle of whatever is going on onboard," said Perunko. Although Catptain Sunny's jobs include holding down the fort while Perunko is off working and overseeing an infinite number of ongoing projects and maintenance that are a daily part of life on a boat, the cat considers his most important task to take place

in the galley, where his job is to sample any food being prepared to make sure it's fit for human consumption, almost akin to being a king's taster.

The Catptain's other chores include making sure that his human colleague checks and fills fresh-water tanks, monitors engine oil levels, and vacuums the boat. While Perunko is working on these tasks, Sunny takes care of another vitally important chore: thoroughly testing newly made-up bunks before company arrives, which can consume hours each day.

Sunny is also required to catch any rodents or bugs that find their way aboard as well as chasing the occasional bird off the boat before it poops on the deck. Perunko says that Sunny also alerts him if something just seems wrong onboard, which is an important responsibility since cats are naturally attuned to even the slightest discrepancy from the norm. To Sunny's credit, Perunko says that the Catptain is keenly aware of what constitutes an unusual noise or vibration on the boat.

Sunny also heads up the welcoming committee and greets every human who steps aboard, whether for an hour or several nights. Sunny sometimes takes this hospitality policy a little too far when he makes his nightly rounds on bed-check duty: the boat's open-cabin-door policy occasionally means that Sunny will insist on sleeping with every guest, at least for a short time. According to Perunko, no one has complained so far.

In his spare time, Sunny also serves as the administrator for a very active Facebook group for seafaring cats called Gatos del Mar, or Cats of the Sea, where he presides over more than two hundred members worldwide and has even helped facilitate a few adoptions. Even with his busy schedule, he rarely misses watching the sunset with Perunko every night up on deck.

However, Sunny considers his most important job — which he takes very seriously and never fails to do — to be relentlessly waking up the breakfast cook, Perunko, at 0615 hours every day to make sure he's taking his job as seriously as Catptain Sunny does.

Exercise Trainer Cat

Fitness experts say that for some folks, the best way to stick to an exercise plan is to schedule regular workouts with your best friend.

Well, since many people's best friends happen to be furry felines, it was no surprise when Catflexing — a fitness routine that involves exercising with a cat or two — first caught fire in the late 1990s. Californian Stephanie Jackson was a longtime fitness buff, and one day when she was working out with dumbbells at home, her cat — a longhaired tortoiseshell named Bad — was determined to help out.

"I was doing my bicep curls and Bad wanted to be held," she said. "I picked her up and started to pump her up and down, and the more I pumped, the more she purred." It didn't hurt that Bad was the perfect weight: Jackson liked to use a five-pound dumbbell for each arm and Bad weighed exactly ten pounds at the time.

Et voilà: Catflexing was born. The feline-powered workout involves a series of standard calisthenics and stretches, but while others might use traditional free weights, pulleys, and ropes, Catflexers use a feline housemate … or two.

Jackson — and Bad — were so taken with their new fitness routine that they worked out almost every day, and Jackson wanted to spread the word. She decided to design a Catflexing calendar to give out for Christmas presents. Each month featured a new exercise and photo of Jackson and Bad working out, and word quickly spread. She and Bad soon had an offer from a book publisher, and the book *Catflexing* hit the bestseller lists. A young Stephen Colbert did a lengthy segment on Catflexing on *The Daily Show* in 1999 and even participated in some of the exercises.

It's important to realize that regardless of the routine a human may pick for a particular day, the final decision is still made by the cat, who, after all, is the primary personal trainer, setting the tone for the day. "A session can last thirty minutes, or it can last two," said Jackson. "It depends on [the cat's] mood. She's the one who thoroughly enjoys it. But if it gets to the point where your cat scratches you, that usually means you weren't listening to her to stop."

Like most personal trainers, Bad has her favorite go-to music to help build energy for the routine. "When Bad hears the disco,

she comes running," said Jackson, who at the same time warned that not every cat would appreciate being used for exercise. In fact, her two other cats prefer to be sedentary, just like many humans. But she does suggest that lovers of other kinds of animals who enjoy keeping fit should give it a try: Dogflexing, snakeflexing, even horseflexing is within the realm of possibility.

"You can do it with any animal," said Jackson. "You can pick up a horse, unless the horse doesn't want to do it, of course. But if they're willing to do it, go for it."

Nurse Cat

Most cats are understandably afraid of veterinarians. But Popeye, a one-eyed cat who lived at the Humane Society of Indianapolis, was so comfortable with veterinarians that he actually joined the staff of the veterinary surgical team that cared for all of the animals that passed through the shelter.

The shelter usually had a surgery cat on staff. The position often provided an unadopted cat a good place to live, though some cats were more skilled at the job than others, just like people. At first, the staff was skeptical that Popeye was up to the job. After all, in addition to losing his eye to a previously untreated injury, the middle-aged brown tabby also had chronic ear infections, skin and fur problems, and dental disease. But he was friendly and curious about new arrivals both human and animal, and because the chances that he'd be adopted were pretty low, the staff decided to give him a trial run.

Happily, Popeye took to his post like he was born to do it, and every day he helped keep animals warm and comfort them while they recovered from surgery.

Popeye's daily routine would start early. After breakfast and a quick nap, he headed for the recovery area outside the surgical suite and lay on the heating mats while he waited for the procedures to start. After each surgery was completed, a vet tech brought the animal out to Popeye so he could cuddle up with each patient. Popeye even had his own special collar tag that read "Surgery Assistant."

His job freed up a human staff member who could then help out with surgical procedures, though the staff admitted that Popeye may have actually contributed to a slight decrease in productivity since they all loved to stop by on their way to and from surgeries and take a few minutes to say hello to him.

Popeye became so skilled at his surgical job that he looked for other ways he could help out, including helping with janitorial duties. Whenever staff and volunteers cleaned out the cat cages, a few bits of kibble tended to fall onto the floor. Popeye would hover nearby and immediately spring into action, removing the stray food almost before it hit the ground.

After two long years of working in surgery, Popeye retired from his job and went to live at a volunteer's home. He was replaced by a new surgical assistant named Morty — short for Voldemort — but the staff missed seeing Popeye on his rounds. "He really had a special gift for speeding the healing process for hundreds of animals coming out of surgery and helping them move through the shelter system and on to their forever homes," said Kristin Conrad, who works at the Humane Society of Indianapolis.

Circus Cat

To those who don't believe that you can train cats, here's an incredible exception: an actual circus where cats leap through the air, jump through barrels, and even play musical instruments, all on cue … at least most of the time.

The Amazing Acro-Cats is a professional full-time cat circus that travels around the United States giving shows, performing for people who can't quite believe what they're seeing. Founder Samantha Martin, who bills herself as chief human and trainer for the feline circus, presides over a rotating roster of cats of all stripes and abilities. Part of her motivation in putting her cats to work is not only to entertain people but also to bring attention to the plight of abandoned and stray cats. After all, all of her employees were formerly orphans, rescues, and strays.

Her first employee was a cat named Tuna. When she was in her twenties, Martin had run a small-scale circus where rats performed tricks, but once she discovered that Tuna was extremely intelligent and eager to learn new things, she started teaching her a few tricks with clicker training, a positive reinforce-

ment program that's typically used to train dogs. "I taught her how to play the guitar and ring a bell," she said. Soon she started training a few of her other cats, who also quickly learned to perform a trick or two, so she put together a small act and called the group The Rock Cats. "People went crazy, so I decided to try and put together a little show that would highlight the skills of each cat and keep them well socialized, mentally sharp, and physically fit," she added.

Though Martin developed a set routine for every show, sometimes the stars veer from the script. "They are pretty much in charge of the show," she admitted. "They really are quite irresponsible, showing up late to practice and changing the lineup of a performance at their whim."

But that's exactly what Acro-Cats fans love, and Martin noted that the things that would get them fired out in the real world are what make them ideal circus employees. Tuna, who has also appeared in ads for Hill's Pet Food and Petco, will occasionally swat fans who come a little too close to her table while she's playing her cowbell during the meet-and-greet after the shows.

Martin sets up a merchandise table before each show so fans can purchase souvenirs, such as catnip toys. Occasionally, one of the cats performing onstage will suddenly head into the audience to rustle through a bag and steal a toy, or decide it's a great time to visit with fans. Wiki—the daredevil of the group—will wander through the rows by walking on everyone's laps, while troublemaker Jax likes to pick one or two members of the audience to visit with and knock over their drinks.

"Many of the cats will leave in the middle of the show and then return later to race across the stage and run up to a platform," she said. "Sometimes a cat will stop to chase another performer, or else leave and come back just in time to do the next trick on the list. You just never know what's going to happen during the show. No two shows are alike because the cats keep things mixed up."

TOYS

POWER RANGERS DELUXE VEHICLE

31360

Security Guard Cat

Picture, for a moment, your typical security guard. If human, you might imagine a big, burly fellow with a bald head and a threatening look on his face. The animal equivalent usually comes in the form of a snarling, muscular breed of dog such as a Rottweiler or a German shepherd, barking menacingly and straining at his leash.

So when Bandai, a Japanese toy company, decided to hire a dainty Bengal cat named Millie to guard its most precious toys at its Southampton warehouse in England in advance of a busy 2012 holiday season, more than a few looked askance at their decision and even mocked the company. Instead of searching for candidates who were more traditional guards, company officials took a counterintuitive route and made a list of qualities that their ideal candidate would possess: superb climbing skills, excellent hearing ability, and a very loud purr, in order to confuse and ultimately fend off any potential bad guys.

"Millie has always had a very vigilant personality and doesn't mind long hours alone," said a company spokesperson. "I'm not surprised she took up a

career as a security guard. The toys are lucky to have such an attentive guardian."

One of the stipulations the company had to meet before Millie agreed to come on board concerned her compensation package: Before she applied her pawprint to the dotted line on the employment contract, Bandai was required to promise her a generous salary in the form of cat food and fish so she could keep up her strength.

Bandai agreed to her stringent demands, and once the ink dried, Millie committed to keeping her end of the bargain, doing a stellar job protecting Alien Creation Transporters and Power Rangers against dangerous intruders, both rodent and human.

Minister Cat

In the early 1980s, a religious order known as the Universal Life Church announced that it would ordain anyone who wanted to serve both God and His people. However, in all their rigorous planning, church authorities never specified the number of legs their ordained ministers should possess.

Good thing, too, because that's precisely how a three-legged brown tabby cat named Sisco from East Belfast, Ireland, came to be known as Reverend Cassidy. Taking the last name of his owner, it wasn't clear if the feline minister had always been called to serve, but with his official certificate of ordination in hand from the church, the furry preacher was fully qualified to preside over weddings, deliver eulogies at funerals, and baptize members of his flock, although this last task was the least favorite part of his job owing to a natural distaste for water.

The Universal Life Church claims not to discriminate against anyone who wants to become a legally ordained minister, regardless of denomination, and the organization's literature says it "opens its doors to all people." Though

many—whether two-, three-, or even four-legged—originally became ordained for the tax benefits, some later saw the profit in performing such ecclesiastical duties as traditionally performed by men and women of the cloth. And if the ministers could be animals, some wondered, why couldn't the congregation? The edict took on a slight twist in the mid-1980s when it was reported that one of Reverend Cassidy's two-legged ordained colleagues by the name of Dawn Rogers had started to conduct weddings for cats, for which the minister charged three hundred dollars a pop.

Though Reverend Cassidy long ago went to kitty heaven, other ULC ministers continue to attend to their four-legged counterparts. But in fact, there seems to be no end to what looks like a growing need for feline ministers: In a nod to *The Big Lebowski*, a denomination called the Church of the Latter-Day Dude tells its ordained clergy that one important way to reach out to their flock is to conduct ceremonies that bless animals during spaying or neutering. When so many people treat their beloved animals like—or even better than—their human children, there's good reason why a similarly ordained cat of the cloth can make it his or her job to officially sanction and preside over the events important to people and the animals in their lives.

Diabetic Alert Cat

When a tuxedo cat named Pippa came to live with the Jansa family in Whitstable, Kent, Great Britain, in 2013, they didn't think they were going to get a hardworking employee along with a family pet. But that's exactly how things turned out.

Daughter Mia, just eight years old when Pippa settled in, was diagnosed with Type 1 diabetes at the age of six. As a result, she's required to monitor her blood sugar levels between four and six times each day and keep syringes filled with insulin nearby in case she suddenly becomes hypoglycemic. Though Pippa wasn't in the habit of sleeping in the girl's bedroom at night, one evening the cat sensed something was wrong. She headed into Mia's room and jumped on her bed to wake her up. When the little girl opened her eyes, Mia realized her blood sugar levels were dangerously low, and she quickly gave herself a shot.

A few nights later, the cat once again suddenly made a beeline for the girl's bedroom and walked on her until Mia woke up. And then on another night, when Mia wouldn't wake up no matter how much Pippa batted at her, the cat ran to the parents' bedroom and me-owed and walked on them until they woke up and followed her as she ran back to the girl's bedroom. By then, both Mia and her parents understood what the cat was doing.

"We quickly realized she was warning us," said Laura Jansa, Mia's mother. "I think it must be something to do with her sense of smell, something to do with the chemistry of Mia's blood changing. Pippa hasn't been trained to do this but obviously senses that there is something wrong and raises the alarm."

Although it's common for dogs to be trained to be alert to a human companion's medical emergencies, medical professionals and people who specialize in training service animals haven't yet tried teaching cats to perform these life-saving duties as well. Though Jansa regularly consults with her daughter's doctors to help decrease Mia's chances of low blood-sugar episodes in the nighttime, she welcomes Pippa's assistance.

"I sleep a bit easier knowing that Pippa is around," she said. "It is so nice to have that backup. It's really reassuring and certainly a bonus we were not expecting. It gives me extra peace of mind to know someone else is keeping an eye on Mia."

Celebrity Cat

From the early days of the World Wide Web, many people have claimed that cats are the main reason why the Internet exists in the first place. Indeed, from Maru, the Japanese cat who loves to sit in boxes, to Keyboard Cat, many feline members of society have gone online and become famous essentially just for being cats.

However, in the world of feline Internet fame, perhaps no cat has gained a higher degree of recognition than Grumpy Cat, aka Tardar Sauce, a mixed-breed cat born on April 4, 2012. According to owner Tabatha Bundesen, Grumpy Cat's rise to fame began when Tabatha's brother Bryan uploaded a short video showing the kitten's permanent scowl when Tardar Sauce was just six months old. Things went a bit nuts from there, with viewers creating online memes featuring Tardar Sauce's picture accompanied by phrases like "I had fun once … It was awful" and "Just put me down." Grumpy Cat was officially born. Bundesen has said that although her cat looks permanently grouchy as the result of dwarfism and a mild underbite, she's a real sweetheart in person.

Before the cat was even a year old, she had appeared on numerous national TV programs, including *Today* and *Good Morning America*, in addition to being voted Most Influential Cat of 2012 by MSNBC. Like many instant Internet sensations, she soon had a book deal. The first Grumpy Cat book was published just after her first birthday. She even had a commercial deal, endorsing Grumppuccino, her own line of caffeinated drinks, available in vanilla, coffee, and mocha flavors. And in late 2014, she starred in her first movie on Lifetime: *Grumpy Cat's Worst Christmas Ever.*

Tardar Sauce hasn't let fame go to her head. Just like other working cats, Tardar Sauce seems to take her job duties in stride, showing up for commercials, photo shoots, and trade show appearances on time all while fulfilling her contractual obligations as Friskies spokescat as well. Her

personal manager, Ben Lashes — who also handles business deals for fellow feline Internet celebrities Keyboard Cat and Nyan Cat — makes sure not to overschedule her, since Tardar Sauce strictly limits her photo sessions to just one each week. But in the end, Grumpy Cat — which is a trademarked name, by the way — holds the final paw of approval on all projects, from the plush toys to movie deals.

Military Working Cat

Though military working dogs have received lots of attention in recent years since news spread that a highly trained soldier dog named Cairo played a part in the raid on Osama bin Laden, few people are aware of the roles that cats have also played in assisting military personnel throughout the years.

At Edwards Air Force Base in California, an active-duty military working cat named Wizzo helps the 95th Mission Support Group protect their equipment from damage in the supply warehouse. Wizzo, a Manx–Maine coon mix, was just over a year old when he was drafted into the service from a nearby pet shelter.

"Wizzo is our mobility rodent deterrent," said Heather Chapman, a warehouse specialist with the battalion. "He was brought in for pest control and is earning his keep by doing his job."

The unit decided to actively recruit a feline soldier when they noticed rodent droppings where the moving supplies and equipment for the unit were being stored. Mice and rats had been chewing holes in them for some time, and though the unit tried a variety of remedies, nothing worked.

"Poison doesn't work inside the warehouse," said Bill Martin, contract manager at the base. "By eating the poison, the rodents just get sick and crawl behind walls and die."

Wizzo solved the problem. Every morning, he greets the first person who comes through the door with his nightly catch, dropping it at their feet as though he is offering them a gift or handing in a homework assignment.

His coworkers keep his kill count posted on a whiteboard at the warehouse. "Whenever anyone starts to doubt his worth, he comes up with another mission completed," Jennifer Starr, 95th MSG mobility lead supervisor, said.

Wizzo has decided to further serve his country by forgoing a paycheck. Instead, his coworkers help to cover his expenses. "Maintaining Wizzo is low cost," said Starr. "Everyone in the supply warehouse contributes by donating supplies and food for him. It is really a team effort."

In addition to his official duties as "weapons systems officer," Wizzo also helps boost staff morale and reduce stress. "He really helps out with the team's morale," Chapman said. "I really love him. If I could, I would take him home."

Alas, unlike his human counterparts, Wizzo's job is 24/7. While his coworkers go home at the end of the day, Wizzo stays behind, always alert to invaders and suspicious critters, proving that in his case at least, a cat's job is never done.

Navy Cat

In addition to serving as military working cats, felines have a long history of living on board naval ships.

According to Oswell Blakeston in his book *Working Cats,* many of the cats who live aboard military ships around the world are highly seasoned sailors. "They will walk down a rope when a ship ties up in harbor and take some shore leave, and they'll be back again before the ship sails," he wrote. "The toughest sailor finds it no disgrace to sentimentalize over the ship's cat."

Perhaps the most famous ship's cat was a black-and-white tuxedo cat by the name of Simon, who served on the British Royal Navy ship the HMS *Amethyst.* Simon took up residence in 1948 while the ship was docked in Hong Kong during the Chinese civil war. A seaman named George Hickinbottom missed his own cat back in England and smuggled him aboard.

Of course, the cat was eventually discovered, but fortunately the ship's commander also had a soft spot for cats, and at the time, rodents had become a serious problem on board. Simon was allowed to stay, and he became a val-

ued seacat. In 1949, the *Amethyst* headed up the Yangtze River to relieve another British ship. Chinese troops opened fire upon the *Amethyst*, which resulted in numerous deaths and injuries.

Immediately after the initial attack, one of the men found the badly injured Simon and brought him to the ship's doctor, who patched him up as best he could. Though he wasn't expected to survive, the cat pulled through and soon resumed his rodenting work.

The ship was trapped on the river for three months due to the ongoing threat of sniper fire, during which Simon's scrappi-

ness and survival helped to boost the morale of the surviving shipmen during the long siege. When the *Amethyst* returned to England, Simon was given a hero's welcome and lauded by the press. Fan mail began to pour in as well as several awards, including the PDSA Dickin Medal from the national charity—The People's Dispensary for Sick Animals—which is given to animals who show great courage and devotion while serving in the military.

Presently, Simon is still the only cat who has ever won the honor since it was established in 1943.

Fast Food Employee Cat

When Pizza Hut Japan decided to throw a spotlight on a few of its feline employees in a series of online commercials, some viewers may have thought they were looking at typical teenage fast-food workers dressed up in little cat suits. After all, the cats—dressed in cute Pizza Hut outfits—were clearly shown acting like the work was beneath them: listlessly pushing a cart of garbage across the floor, opening the cash register by mistake and just staring at it in response, and falling asleep on the job.

The ads, released in the summer of 2014, played on the Japanese expression *"Neko no te mo karitai"*—loosely translated as "You want to borrow a cat's paw"—which means you're so busy and overworked that you'd even accept help from a cat.

"Call Pizza Hut when you don't have time to prepare a meal, and our super cats will help you out," said Yuko Koki, a company spokesperson. But based on the jobs that the feline employees perform in the ads, if these cats are working on the clock when you place your order, you may be waiting a long time. Each

ad shows a cat performing a different function, from planning a delivery to ~~answering~~ ignoring a ringing phone, and even checking inventory, with varying degrees of success. "What you see actually are cats doing nothing but just being cats," Koki admitted.

While the ads were running, more than a few customers were disappointed when they placed an order and a real live human showed up to deliver their pizza instead of one of the cats.

The names and backstory that the company developed for each cat are both funny and revealing: Tencho, which means "store manager" in Japanese, is a Scottish Fold who was born in downtown Tokyo. His lifelong dream was to own his own store, but he's settled for bossing the others around.

Detch — or Trainee — was born in the back of a gas station. He used to be a gang leader but has reformed and now takes great pride in his job as pizza delivery driver. Hime — aka Princess — is also a Scottish Fold and the only female on the team. She was born in New York on Wall Street and has a New York accent when she meows. Dora — whose name means "bad" in Japanese — is the Bohemian of the group and doesn't talk much about his past. A former stray, he is a much bigger pizza fan than the other members of his team.

The cats were actually hired and trained by an animal model agency, but art tends to imitate life: "Tencho is the team leader, and it's funny that even in real life during the video shoot, the other cats were afraid of him," said Koki.

Theater Cat

Cats of all stripes have a lengthy history of working in the theater, both on stage and behind the scenes.

For centuries, cats have been employed in theaters as Directors of Rodent Control. Auditions were typically conducted in nearby alleys and yards, a feline kind of Schwab's drugstore where anyone could be discovered. The payoff was a warm place to sleep with all the vermin they could consume. And sometimes these workers found their way onstage when a play called for a feline to fill in a walk-on role. But in recent decades, as the theater world got more serious about picking its human actors, the same thing happened with regard to animal thespians. Aside from the occasional open audition, producers and directors increasingly relied on animal talent agencies for their feline performers. But despite theaters opting for seasoned actors, it's clear that just like their human counterparts, theater cats are not immune to delivering flubbed lines or developing a serious case of last-minute nerves.

Back in the fall of 2009, a longhaired orange cat by the name of Jasper

had his theatrical debut at the ripe old age of fourteen when *Breakfast at Tiffany's* played at the Theatre Royal Haymarket in London. Director Sean Mathias said that Jasper — an experienced feline actor with a résumé that included several films — was the consummate professional. "He had the right look and temperament, and he seemed like he was really Holly's cat," said Mathias, adding that Jasper strongly resembled the cat that author Truman Capote described in his novella as belonging to Holly Golightly, the carefree young socialite and the star of the story.

At the same time, anxiety is always high when an animal has a crucial role in a play, no matter the hours of training beforehand.

"You can have heart attacks with animals," said Mathias. "They can upstage the actors terribly."

So it's no surprise that sometimes things go horribly wrong. One night, Jasper wasn't feeling up to snuff, and his understudy, a white cat named Bob with a fluffy orange tail, went on in his place. In the play, there's an important point where Holly pushes the cat away. Unfortunately, Bob must have gotten nervous, because when it was time for his big moment, instead of heading offstage and away from the actress, he stuck by her side, drawing big laughs from the audience, which wasn't what author Truman Capote had in mind.

Library Cat

When two librarians in the small town of Minden, Nevada, decided to hire two Scottish Fold cats to help control the rodent population in their brand-new building, they were honoring an age-old tradition of librarians everywhere, from their counterparts in eighteenth-century England to ancient Greece, who kept cats on the payroll to prevent damage to both building and books.

However, the cats that Jan Louch and Yvonne Saddler brought on board and named Baker and Taylor not only protected the books from hungry mice, but they also started moonlighting as the much-loved mascots for Baker & Taylor, a book wholesaling company that at the time had been in business for 150 years. Through their ads, posters, and the ubiquitous book bags, the pair became famous all over the world while increasing the company's bottom line and making librarians and booksellers all over the world happy.

"At first, people couldn't believe we had the nerve to let a couple of cats live in the library," said Louch. But it didn't take long before the patrons became used to the sight of two cats with funny ears wandering around the library, supervising staff at the circulation desk and hopping up onto the tables in the reading room to sit on the exact

spot in a magazine, book, or newspaper that a patron wanted to read.

Everyone who visited the library fell in love with the cats, from the teenagers who liked to pet Taylor with one hand while turning the pages of a book with the other to the older, arthritic patrons who got down on their knees to rub Baker's belly as he lay stretched out on his back inside the lobby. The cats helped raise the spirits of the library staff, too.

Fans traveled from far and wide to see the cats in person, and they were richly rewarded when they saw Baker holding court at the circulation desk and Taylor in his usual sitting-up pose. The moment that Louch stamped their posters with the cats' official "pawtograph" was, of course, the icing on the cake.

Even though the cats died almost twenty

years ago, librarians and booksellers are still known to break into heated arguments at trade shows and conventions if: (a) they reach the Baker & Taylor booth after the complimentary book bags have run out, and/ or (b) they miss the chance to pose with the human-sized Baker & Taylor cats (i.e., two adults wearing costumes). And the posters of the two Scottish Folds still adorn the walls of thousands of bookstores and librar-

ies around the world.

Even today, people in Minden still talk about the cats, and librarians from elsewhere still visit the library to honor two cats for a job well done.

Cat Burglar Cat

Jean Chu and Jim Coleman of San Mateo, California, have heard more than their fair share of cat burglar jokes. That's because Dusty, the Snowshoe cat they adopted in 2006, became famous for doing a job that would get him thrown in jail if he had two legs instead of four and wasn't covered with fur.

Almost every night, Dusty goes on the prowl in their suburban neighborhood and steals a hodgepodge of clothing and household items from his neighbors, bringing everything home so he can present his finds as gifts to his family. His nightly activities have rightfully earned him the nickname of Klepto Kitty.

"I think he saw a need to clean up the neighborhood because he didn't like to see things just lying around," said Chu. Over the years, Dusty has brought home rags, gloves, towels, car wash mitts, balloons, children's shoes and socks, stuffed toys, and even swimming gear. In other words, anything that might be left outside in a front or back yard that was also easy enough for a normal-size cat to drag for a block or so in the middle of the night.

According to Chu, Dusty is most active in the summer and fall, when the

weather is warm, which is also the time of year when people tend to leave their property lying around outside. In fact, when winter rolled around during his first year on the job, Dusty went on hiatus from November through January. Chu and Coleman thought Dusty had quit his life of crime. But once the weather started to warm up a little and neighbors started to be careless with their outdoor items again, the cat eagerly got back to work.

Dusty has a counterpart named Oscar in Southampton, England. Though he started his job by innocently bringing home a pair of socks, the ginger tabby soon developed a preference for ladies' underwear, though he has also stolen a pair of gardening gloves, kneepads, and even a paint roller.

"Oscar was very proud that he had found these presents for us and would drop them at our feet," said Peter Weismantel, who rescued the twelve-year-old cat with his wife Birgitt at Christmas 2009. "I know it's in a cat's nature to bring stuff back to their 'den,' and we've had some who have brought in mice. At first we thought it was just rubbish he'd found, but then the quality started improving, including a pair of brand-new pants. We had no idea where he was getting them from and at first we thought it would just go away, but it began to escalate.

He'd think nothing of bringing two or three things back each day."

Weismantel contacted the police in case his neighbors were reporting thefts, but the officer brushed off his concerns. In the meantime, Oscar continued with his crime spree. Instead of throwing away the cat's finds, Weismantel decided to store the cat burglar's nightly haul in the garage just in case a neighbor came looking for their undies.

Police Cat

On the flip side, it's important to realize that cats are fully capable of serving on both sides of the law.

Though you wouldn't think that cats could help fight crime, there's a brown-and-white tabby cat in Japan who goes above and beyond law enforcement techniques to help bring in the bad guys while building goodwill among local residents.

Officer Iemon — pronounced "ee-eh-mon" — was just a stray newborn kitten when he was rescued in April 2011. One of the officers at the Yoro Station in Kyoto found him abandoned nearby, brought him home, made sure he was okay, and then decided to put him to work.

The police ordered a custom-made uniform for the cat, and just like his human colleagues, once Iemon puts on his uniform, he immediately becomes serious and shifts into law enforcement mode, ready to help fight any crime that may occur on his watch.

Almost one-third of the local population is over the age of sixty-five, and

the officers wanted to teach older residents how to protect themselves against a common phone scam where the caller pretends to be a relative and asks for money. A sergeant was already visiting the senior residents in the neighborhood to conduct investigations and reassure them, and Iemon started to accompany him as he made his rounds.

The feline officer soon proved to be so popular with residents that local schools and community organizations invited him to help present traffic-safety and crime-stopper workshops at kindergartens and elementary classes.

Though most people loved to see Iemon, a few residents were initially suspicious of the cat since his name is similar to *Goemon,* which is the name of a legendary thief in Japan. But after the doubters met him and saw his official uniform and cap, any suspicions about his true nature were dispelled.

When he's not out on patrol or participating in presentations, Officer Iemon prefers to sit on the desk at the main entrance where he can keep an eye on people coming and going. And he's taken a lesson from his human colleagues by currying favor with high-ranking police officials whenever they visit.

Since he first joined the force, Officer Iemon has significantly helped bolster the national effort to help fight crime not only in Kyoto but all over Japan. As a result, people from other parts of the country have started to visit the cat in person, giving him so many treats that his fellow officers had to put him on a diet. Sadly, Officer Iemon had to cut down on those catnip doughnuts.

Distillery Cat

Distilleries in Scotland have a long history of employing cats to help protect the premises from birds and mice; after all, the mash that eventually turns up as fine smoky whisky sold at some very high prices starts its life as a simple mixture of barley and water. It doesn't take long for birds and mice to come calling.

Which is why Glenturret, Scotland's longest-operating distillery, was home to a champion feline employee named Towser, who made it into the *Guinness Book of World Records* after having a documented kill of precisely 28,899 mice over his tenure.

Distilleries in the United States have followed the trend of keeping cats on the payroll. At Maker's Mark in Loretto, Kentucky, a feline by the name of Whisky Jean was originally hired to keep tabs on the local rodent population, but from the start she turned into a real go-getter, adding to her workload without being asked. For one, she took the initiative to become an active team member at the visitor center, where guests gather before tours and later to pur-

chase additional bottles as mementos to bring home.

Over the course of a typical workday, Whisky Jean has a full schedule, greeting visitors and supervising ticket sales. During break time, she does her regular stretching routine and drinks from the faucet in the staff room for hydration.

She also squeezes in a side gig as a model, since she's photographed many times every day. "As the human minders of cats at Scottish distilleries have discovered, feline staffers not only help with rodent prevention, but also play an active role in helping to market the distillery," said Jacklyn Evans, spokeswoman for Maker's Mark. "People post tons of pictures of her on social media, while other visitors pet and hold her. We even have visitors who send her presents and toys."

As a result, Whisky Jean's human coworkers have come to forgive some of her foibles, from climbing on the register keyboard in the middle of a busy day to chasing birds on the roof of the distillery.

Cat Café Cat

Ask anyone who works with the public: It can be tough to deal with different kinds of people all day long. Having to smile and be diplomatic with a difficult customer all while standing on your feet for most of your shift explains why turnover is so high in the retail and hospitality businesses.

It's no different for working cats either, though the feline employees at a cat café admittedly have it a bit easier. After all, if you're the primary reason why people come through the door, customers will understandably cut you a bit of slack for doing exactly what you were born to do: shed, purr a little, and offer up your head for an occasional scratch. You might even fall asleep on the job for hours each day or totally ignore the customers. But the patrons who come in for a spot of tea or a foamy cappuccino for a break in their day don't seem to mind: They're just happy to be able to spend time with the cats.

Typically, at a cat café patrons pay a set entrance fee and then shell out extra depending upon what kind of food or drink they want. Some cafés also allow customers to purchase cat food and treats for the feline employees, but

many cafés prohibit this to ensure that the cats don't become obese.

The first cat café actually opened in Taiwan in 1998, but it wasn't until one opened in Japan—in Osaka in 2004—that the concept really caught on. The cat is close to a sacred being in Japan, but many residents are prohibited from keeping cats at home because of space constraints and housing regulations. By 2014, Tokyo alone would be home to forty cat cafés, and cats around the world could find employment at cafés in Spain, Great Britain, and even the United States.

Though social skills and the ability to get along with people—even for a short time—are indeed valuable talents, some cat cafés hire felines not so much for their special abilities as for their physical appearances, as is the case in many retail stores. At some cat cafés, employees are strictly purebreds—in Japan, a favorite breed is the Scottish Fold—while the feline employees at Lady Dinah's Cat Emporium in London are all rescued from shelters. Although you can't take an employee home from Dinah's on a permanent basis, a few cat cafés that draw their entire feline staff from local shelters do allow patrons to adopt an employee … or two.

News Anchor Cat

Despite their off-the-cuff appearances, news programs that feature a panel of hosts, anchorpersons, and a mix of rotating guests are typically highly scripted productions where even the tiniest unplanned word or action can throw the show and staff into a frantic tizzy.

Of course, cats are not known for paying much attention to following someone else's schedule. So when famous Japanese journalist Yasuhiro Tase launched a political news program in the spring of 2008 hosted by himself and two other anchors, some questioned his wisdom when he decided to add a fourth anchor to the show in the form of a buff orange American Shorthair named Mago.

But Tase had a plan for his show, *Politics Right Now with Yasuhiro Tase*, a weekly digest of national and international news: He wanted political guests to soften up during discussions on the live show. And having a cat stroll by at inopportune moments would pretty much ensure that this would happen.

Mago's job required him to spend the day in the studio with Tase and

his guests, both on camera and off. Once the cameras started to roll during the live broadcast, Mago got to work. He'd occasionally stop at a certain point on the desk, blocking a flip chart that one of the anchors was pointing at to describe some detail. Other times, the cat would lie down right beneath the display, making it look as if he wanted viewers to look at the board at that exact moment. And when the cameraman zoomed in for a close-up of a guest, Mago would choose that moment to walk right in front of the camera, blocking the person entirely, while at other times he'd stand near the camera but only the tip of his tail would appear in the shot.

"Imagine seeing a cat tail crossing the TV screen during an intense political discussion," said producer Kyoko Komatsuzawa. "Mago did way more than we expected."

As a result, Mago's presence did cause guests to loosen up. Some viewers reported that the only time they've seen certain politicians smile was on the show. It didn't take long for the program to become known as "The Show with the Cat," and viewership grew steadily as word spread. Soon an increasing number of previously camera-shy politicians contacted the producers to appear on the show.

On any news program, the production staff pays a lot of attention to guests, fawning over them and catering to their every whim. Apparently, Mago never got that memo. When former Japanese prime minister Yasuhiro Nakasone appeared on the show, both anchors and staff were visibly nervous, falling all over themselves to attend to his needs. In contrast, Mago was a veritable island of calm, sauntering past Nakasone on camera to get a few scratches and head pats before proceeding to stick his head into the prime minister's mug for a few sips of tea in front of an audience of millions.

Unfortunately, Mago passed away unexpectedly in the fall of 2014 from a heart condition, and coanchor Miki Handa delivered a tearful eulogy of the cat on the program. Mourners showed up by the thousands and wrote online notes of condolence. Some wondered whether the program would add another feline coanchor, and happily producers filled the job with a calico kitten named Nyanya later that year.

Musician Cat

Though most cats will vocally produce a variety of musical tones over the course of the day—either prompted or totally spontaneous—there are a growing number of felines who actually create and perform their own original compositions.

First off is a five-cat band in Japan by the name of Musashi. They first hit the airwaves with their version of "Jingle Bells" in 2007, which received 275,000 views on YouTube Japan the first week before the video went viral worldwide. The cats soon signed with a Japanese promotion company—their contract specified that for every song they composed, each cat would be paid with a full-size skipjack tuna—and began appearing on TV shows and writing theme songs for music videos and TV programs.

Another feline musician who became famous via the Internet is Nora the Piano Cat, who lives with her human personal assistants, artist Burnell Yow! and piano teacher Betsy Alexander, in Philadelphia. One day the rescued cat sat down at the grand piano and began to play. Soon Nora was hooked, prac-

ticing every day and even helping out during Betsy's piano lessons. In early 2007, the couple decided to upload a video to YouTube in which the feline prodigy showed off her musical talents. Within months, the video had almost eight million views, and Nora was on her way.

Since her debut, Nora has authored two books—one on how humans can improve their musical skills and one for children—and has conducted countless interviews with media around the world. A Lithuanian composer wrote a catcerto specifically for Nora, who graciously performed the world premiere via video.

According to Alexander, Nora hasn't let success go to her head, and she still puts in a fair amount of practice each day and helps supervise piano lessons. "She considers it her moral imperative to play duets with my students to help them with their powers of musical concentration," said Alexander. "In fact, at times she can be rather overenthusiastic in her desire to play, in which case I am forced to pull the bench away from the piano. It's the only way to get her to stop playing, because she only plays from a seated position. She simply refuses to walk on the keys."

Alexander has received e-mails from piano teachers who admit that Nora plays better than some of their students. Some teachers have referred to her sensitive touch and are impressed that she never bangs on the keys. A piano pedagogy professor even used Nora in a video about proper technique.

But despite the constant accolades of a high-level musical career, the life of a feline musician is both rigorous and demanding. As much as Nora enjoys this rare and extraordinary job, it is not an easy path for a cat. "After all, she has only two paws and not ten fingers," said Alexander. And all the fan adulation can be daunting to a cat with such a penchant for privacy.

"But she is an ambassador for the brilliance of cats in general and their ability to succeed at anything they put their mind to," Alexander continued. "She clearly enjoys being an inspiration to others and believes that everyone should learn to play an instrument, as she is certain that learning an instrument makes everyone smarter."

Writer's Muse Cat

Writers and cats have long been associated with each other, serving as companion and inspiration. Writers both famous and obscure have worked with cats on their shoulders and laps.

Millions of cats have undoubtedly walked across millions of computer and typewriter keyboards and have teethed on tens of thousands of pens. Cats generally do their best to distract an author from her true calling to allow the designated human can opener to focus on what's really important: their feline selves.

Luminaries from William S. Burroughs to Anaïs Nin claimed they couldn't write a word without having at least one cat around, and preferably more. And the descendants of Ernest Hemingway's polydactyl cats still roam around his Key West property, and probably still at his Cuba residence where it's estimated that he once shared his home with fifty-seven felines.

The late Edward Gorey was famous for having a house full of cats who occasionally ran roughshod over his desk while he was working. "My cats have influenced me a great deal, but I can say I have no idea what they're thinking about," he admitted. "They're obviously attuned to something we're not, and there's something about them that's utterly remote from people, and I find that kind of nice."

William S. Burroughs was known for his close relationships with cats, and toward the end of his life penned a free-form book entitled *The Cat Inside*. He credited his feline companions with much more than inspiration: "My relationship with my cats has saved me from a deadly pervasive ignorance."

Or maybe they just want a byline or at least coauthor credit after years of serving as muse and inspiration to writers and authors throughout the centuries. In her poem "Miao," the poet Dilys Laing ruminated on this possibility:

I put down my book, The Meaning of Zen,
And see the cat smiling into her fur as she
delicately combs it with her rough pink tongue.
"Cat, I would lend you this book to study
but it appears you have already read it."
She looks up and gives me her full gaze.
"Don't be ridiculous," she purrs, "I wrote it."

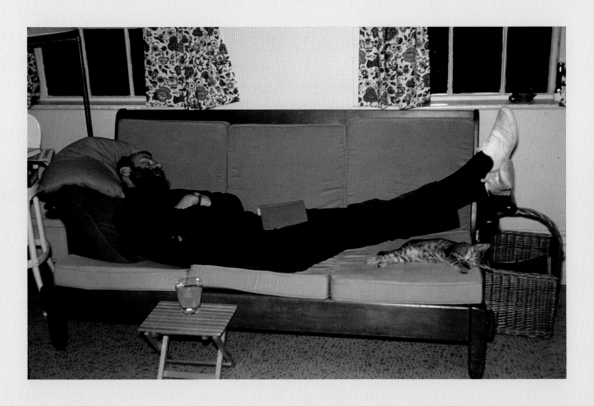

Model Cat

Any model will tell you that the job is a lot harder than it looks. Oh sure, twisting and smiling and sashaying in front of the camera may seem like child's play, but looking good on cue is tough for many humans, especially if you aren't in the mood to follow somebody else's orders.

Which automatically applies to most cats. The upside for feline models, though, is that there's always the potential to upstage any humans who also appear in the picture. Cat models — professional and amateur — are highly skilled and incredibly versatile, whether they're posing for a cat food ad or donning a tiny costume or wig. It's not just humiliating, it's also hard to look good on camera when a model's first impulse is to scratch and wriggle until the accessory or article of clothing finally falls off.

Catnip may help in easing the pain — both during the photo shoot as well as afterward — but the truth is that temperament is as important as good looks for a feline model, maybe even more so. Perhaps the most famous feline model of the Internet age is Prin, a snow-white Scottish Fold, who Japanese

designer Takako Iwase employs to feature her handmade costumes. It helps that Prin is an extremely mellow cat, and also that Iwase works to charm her on each photo shoot in the same way that human photographers coo at their models in order to bring out the best in them.

"Cats love to be complimented," said Iwase. "You've got to be like, 'OH MY GOD, you are so CUTE, you're the best cat EVER!!' and they will actually feel it and feel better about wearing the clothes."

Another famous feline model is Nesta of Nesta's Nest, an Etsy store featuring hats for cats, who first became known when posing with a hat that made her look like a lion. Yumiko Landers, who launched her store in 2012, said that the lion hat is a natural choice for any cat, even if they resist it at first. "Every cat we've ever known believes they're

the master of their domain, so I thought there's no better way to represent that than making them look like a true lion," she said, adding that without Nesta, she doesn't think her business would have been as successful.

"The customers love Nesta," said Landers. "Some even think he's not our cat but a professional model. They're absolutely amazed how well he models the hat without any training whatsoever."

Other well-seasoned cat models include Petunia and siblings Jitters and Justus, feline models at Cushzilla, a company that sells everything from wigs for cats to cow costumes for dogs. Spouses and business partners Leah Workman and Hiroshi Hibino acknowledge that a cat modeling session is so difficult that even bribing their own cats with treats often isn't enough. Indeed, they are always actively looking for new faces.

But Workman warns aspiring feline models that posing is a lot harder than it sounds, especially for the humans working with them.

"New models can be exhausting," she warns. "They absolutely don't know their angles yet, they run and hide wigs behind sofas, and they gleefully disrobe before the money shot, which can be highly vexing."

In addition, Hibino was afraid if he asked the cats to do something even mildly unpleasant that they'd hate him and Workman. Indeed, that first day was a tough slog, awkward and sweaty, resulting in more than a few photos of blurry, streaky blobs.

The second — and subsequent — days of the photo shoot went much smoother. "The cats ran toward the box of costumes and wigs instead of away from it," said Workman. "Dressing up had turned into a game to play with us, rather than the awkward reluctance and downright hostility one might expect from a bewigged feline."

According to Workman, Jitters likes wearing the pilot suit so much that he believes he *is* Captain Jitters. "His favorite game is to jump into a cardboard box and have Hibino lift him up and fly him around the house," she said. "I love him in the crazy cat lady wig myself, but I think the concept of a cat-hoarding cat is funny. I've seen how Jitters will take all his toys and put them in his cat house, and that's how hoarding starts."

Furniture Tester Cat

Most domestic cats are constantly warned against scratching the furniture, but two lucky cats in Grand Rapids, Michigan — a Desert Lynx named Ickle and a Bengal/Siamese mix named Heisenberg — are not only not shooed away from the furniture, they're encouraged to scratch, bite, and jump on it, as often as possible.

That's because these cats work as testers and designers at Catastrophi-Creations, where human owners Mike Wilson and Megan Hanneman sell everything from cat bridges and shelves to fabric-covered feline "playplaces." It all started when the couple brought home their first cat, Ickle. In addition to purchasing the requisite dishes and litter box, they bought a couple of cat trees and thought that a rope bridge would make it easy for the cat to travel from one tree to the next.

The cat enjoyed it so much that they not only opened an Etsy store to sell the bridge to other cat lovers, they also started to design new pieces. But they needed to beef up their staff, so they interviewed and hired another feline co-

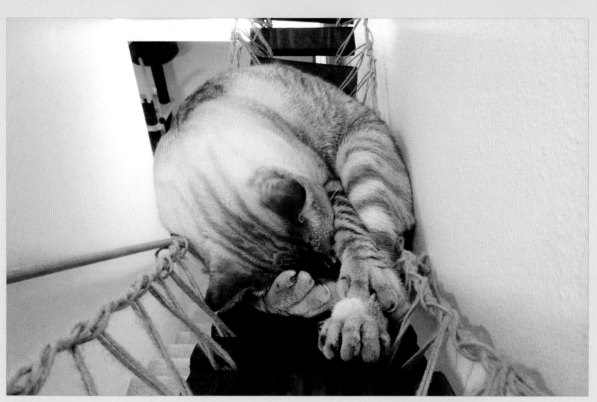

worker named Heisenberg, who turned out to complement Ickle perfectly.

When Ickle turned a year old, he suddenly started to put on weight, which made him pretty lazy. But Wilson and Hanneman didn't mind, because they considered it to be a valuable job skill, since the furniture has to be continually tested for napping and reclining purposes. Heisenberg, on the other hand, is the more slender and energetic of the two, so he was put in charge of testing any new products that required a little more wear and tear before they could be put on the market.

Until very recently, the company was run from Wilson and Hanneman's home, but the feline employees were making it difficult for the human staff to get actual work done, creating a tag team of harassment aimed at their two-legged coworkers. During his copious amounts of break time, Heisenberg would lurk on one of the corner cat shelves mounted high up on a wall and swat at the humans whenever they walked by, creating a potential workman's comp situation. Then, after Heisenberg unnerved them, Ickle would take over, dashing in front of the first human he spotted walking through the office before stopping short in front of their feet and flipping over onto his back, angling for a few belly rubs. Wilson and Hanneman had no choice but to give in because after all, playing and belly rubs are the cats' primary form of compensation.

But they eventually decided to move the business into a more traditional office setting. Wilson admitted that he sometimes felt guilty because of the pressure of his feline cofounders' jobs. "They really never end," he lamented. "They work 24/7, whether playing or sleeping on our furniture." The schedule becomes especially breakneck in the months leading up to December, when the cats are frantically testing new items to sell during the all-important holiday season.

In late 2014, the company hired a third feline employee, a calico kitten named Lylah, to help out. "She has her own style and is bringing a new, frenetic energy to the workplace," said Wilson, adding that as Ickle and Heisenberg start interacting with the rookie, they're all figuring out new ways to use the company's products, which is sure to lead to lots of new and exciting items.

Artist Cat

Back in the 1990s, the phenomenon of cats who exercised their artistic creativity through painting was first publicized in the bestselling book *Why Cats Paint*. Written in a dry academic fashion, accompanied by profiles and photos of a variety of cats working at easels, more than a few people had no idea it was a total spoof.

But in New South Wales, Australia, there's a group of cats who actually do paint and have received international acclaim. Louise Clayton and her daughter, Tegan Ellis, run an animal rescue service, and in 2012 they decided to put their rescued cats to work by creating paintings which could then be sold to raise money to help save even more abandoned and orphaned pets.

The result: Rescue Cat Art — home of the Pawcasso cats. The project "allowed the cats to express their new lease on life through paintings as well as putting a small dent into the enormous vet bill," said Clayton, who, with her daughter, set out a couple of canvases and some nontoxic paint and waited for a trio of cats named Mini, Mouse, and Sabu to find inspiration.

It didn't take long.

"We put paint out for them and they walked across and played with balls we put out," said Ellis. "They delighted in the fact they could place their paws on the canvas and it would become squishy under them. It's just a bit messy because once they finish they just wander off."

Of course, there were the inevitable mishaps when the cats missed the canvas completely and landed on the floor, leaving a slippery splash of color on the linoleum. And cleaning up after each artistic session was not an easy task.

But the cats loved their new jobs, and after the paintings were featured on the cats' Facebook page and at local art fairs and fundraisers, people started to buy up the feline art, which leaned toward the abstract. Since Ellis and Clayton also care for several dogs at home, it didn't take long before they started to think about putting the canine members of the household to work too, which may well lead to a sequel: *Why Dogs Paint*.

Hotel Concierge Cat

Many small inns and bed-and-breakfasts have a resident cat to help guests feel at home. But the famed Algonquin Hotel in New York City takes the concept one step further by having a feline assist in the role of concierge.

The hotel has a long history of having a cat serve as the DirectFUR of Guest Relations. Since the 1930s, when the first feline assumed the role, a total of ten cats have held the job — all but one have been rescues — and to make it easy on long-time guests, all of the males have been named Hamlet while the three females have all been called Matilda.

All DirectFURs are required to not only greet guests and make them feel warm and welcome, but also to help supervise the bell staff. To this end, the current DirectFUR — Matilda — spends much of her time camped out on the bell cart, swishing her tail for attention and occasionally losing her balance when the bellmen hoist heavy bags onto the cart. She also presides over the annual Cat Fashion Show at the hotel, which raises thousands of dollars each year for local shelters and rescues.

Matilda's job description also calls for her to spend a good chunk of her workday fast asleep, a skill at which she excels. Her people skills are stellar: Most guests love to meet her and a few pet her and pose for selfies with her. After eight decades of having a cat at the front desk, the current Matilda enjoys an international following, and people travel from all over the world to see her. In fact, some visitors will come in to say hello even if they're staying at another hotel in the city. She was recently humbled when a heart transplant recipient came to see her as part of her bucket list.

Matilda number three almost didn't make it past her first day on the job: She stole one of the night manager's shoes so he was forced to stand up and go look for it. Once his chair was unoccupied, the hotel's newest employee nestled right into it and refused to budge. But she got a pass, because in the hospitality business such quick thinking comes in handy at a busy hotel where staff must always be anticipating a guest's next request and know how to fulfill it. Matilda was forgiven and she quickly settled in for a lengthy tenure, to the delight of both guests and staff.

"It's wonderful seeing guests' faces when they first see Matilda," said hotel spokesman Nicholas Sciammarella. "Some are so surprised that they start calling home right there in the lobby: 'Honey, guess what? They have a cat here!' I think she brings a bit of home and warmth to everyone."

Weather Observer Cat

Cats have long been known to forecast the weather. A couple of old wives' tales say that rain is on the way if a cat sneezes or washes behind an ear, or that a bad storm is imminent whenever a cat snores.

So it's no surprise that the forecasters at New Hampshire's Mount Washington Observatory have long relied on cats to help do their jobs. Perched on top of the highest peak in the Northeast, it's been called "Home of the World's Worst Weather." The observatory first opened on the summit in 1932, and cats have been an essential part of life at 6,288 feet, serving alongside human weather observers throughout extremely long winters and entertaining visitors during the all-too-short summers.

From the beginning, cats were the best and only defense against rodents in the headquarters, which back then was really nothing more than a wooden shack. As the only warm building on a very cold summit, it served as a beacon to those hardy vermin that managed to make it to the mountaintop. While eight cats worked on the summit in the early days, today only one feline em-

ployee is needed, since the current building, built in 1980, is much sturdier and less susceptible to rodents.

In recent history, the most famous feline employees have been a calico cat named Inga — her frosted-whiskers picture postcard made her famous — and Nin, whose white fur bore black patches. Marty is the current summit cat and was hired in 2008 because the staff figured that a black Maine coon cat would be easy to spot against the snow.

Mike Carmon, education specialist and weather observer, has worked alongside Marty ever since. "Marty is a great way for our members and fans to relate to our mountaintop weather station as not only a place of work, but also a home for the weather observers," he said.

In summertime, Marty spends most of his shift outdoors, visiting with tourists and getting plenty of exercise out on the rocks. During winter, however, like his human coworkers, he rarely goes outside, and takes great pride in assisting the night staff with weather observations throughout the graveyard shift.

Carmon brings educational programs about weather and the summit to classrooms around the country via videoconference, and depending upon his mood, Marty will help out. Though he doesn't like to stay in front of the camera for long, during one presentation Marty started playing with one of his toys during the program, scampering back and forth behind Carmon as he talked. Carmon was oblivious to being upstaged until he heard the student viewers laughing.

"Marty definitely attracts people who may not be otherwise interested in a mountaintop weather station," he said. For staff, he's a great companion since all of the observers are away from their families, friends, and pets for a week at a time while on shift. After all, Marty is the only staff member who never leaves the summit.

Just like his human coworkers, at the end of a long, hard day of work, Marty heads to the living quarters and plops down on the couch to relax a little until it's time to go back and watch the sky.

Tour Guide Cat

Most cats are not known as being particularly eager to jump into a car, train, or plane. But two cats in Japan enjoy the open road so much that Jalan, a travel company, hired them to serve as tour guides and ambassadors, encouraging people to travel not only throughout Japan but around the world.

Seasoned traveler Nyalan — "nya" translates to "meow" in Japanese — and his younger apprentice, Deshi, both travel carrying tiny suitcases around their necks. Photos and videos posted on the Jalan Web site and the company's social media accounts show the feline companions in a variety of settings, from rural hot springs to the passenger compartment of a bullet train, designed to give travelers ideas for their own trips. Through their human translators, they also answer questions from readers and give advice.

Nyalan actually started traveling in 2007 by himself, appearing in brief videos that showed him staying in luxury hotels, visiting spas, and even getting an in-room massage. In 2012, Jalan decided Nyalan needed a travel buddy and brought on Deshi as the slightly hyperactive counterpart to Nyalan's mel-

low Zen master. Accordingly, the focus of the travel itinerary changed and took on a more adventurous flair: The Web site shows the pair traveling on trains, hiking and fishing, and shopping for souvenirs, always with Nyalan in the role of mentor, while Deshi follows along like a young disciple, soaking up the older cat's experience and knowledge.

According to a Jalan spokesperson, the first Nyalan retired after a few years, and Deshi—now an experienced traveler with tens of thousands of miles under his belt—morphed into Nyalan II. A new Deshi was brought on board after a rigorous interview process, and production of new videos and Web stories commenced.

Nyalan I, who believed you could never stop learning, continued to travel after he retired, and Nyalan II followed his mentor's example and recently started to teach himself how to be a better travel photographer, in order to improve both his own trips and provide an example to his many fans.

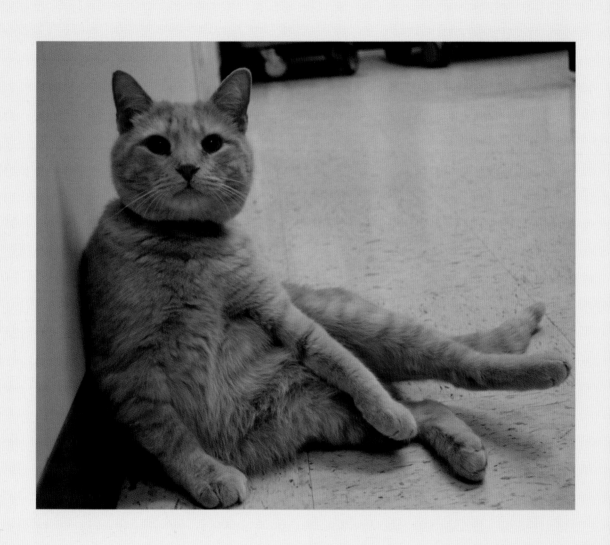

Hospice Cat

In 2010, a remarkable book called *Making Rounds with Oscar* was published. It told the story of a brown-and-white-striped tabby cat who lived in a Rhode Island nursing home and became famous worldwide for his ability to not only soothe patients and staff, but to zero in on those who were in their last hours and spend time with them until they passed.

Though this doesn't seem like a common feline occupation, the staff at a hospice unit at a VA hospital in Salem, Virginia, thought otherwise. Shortly after she finished reading the book, physician assistant Laura Hart began to rally colleagues around the idea of hiring an Oscar of their own, if not specifically to help patients move from one world to the next. She thought that having a resident feline on staff would help make everyone feel just a little bit better on a daily basis.

Office manager Lisa Tyree began the interview process at a local shelter. After meeting a good-natured orange tabby cat named Tom, she knew she'd found her new employee. When he arrived in April 2012, he got right to work, spending his days visiting hospice veterans as well as those under nursing home care.

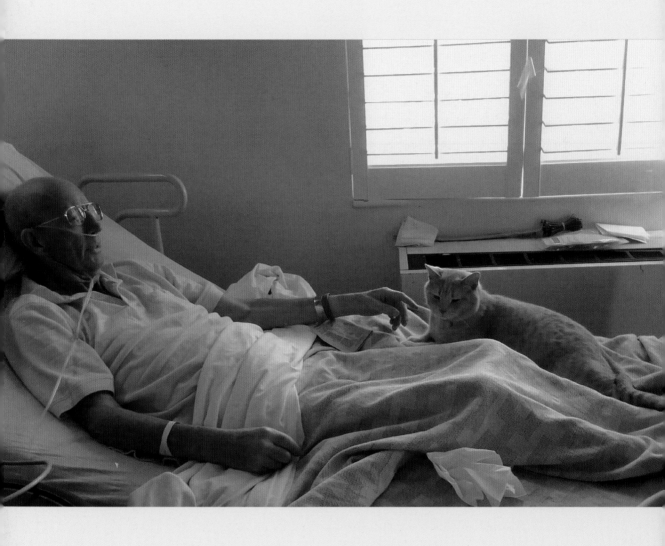

"Tom has known what to do since the first day he was here," said Hart.

In addition to visiting with long-time patients, Tom is in charge of welcoming new veterans to the unit and likes to wander into the room within a few minutes of a new veteran's arrival. When he isn't curled up on a bed or chair in a patient's room, Tom often patrols the halls to help boost staff morale. Tom never misses the unit's twice-weekly team meetings, and he's been known to scratch on the closed door demanding to be let in if they start without him.

"Having Tom here helps makes it seem less like a hospital and more like a home," said Dorothy Rizzo, palliative care coordinator. "He normalizes sometimes very difficult circumstances and provides a distraction from the reality of being in a hospital."

Tom also helps to comfort family members. "Having a cat in the room will take your mind off what's going on," said Hart. "He'll do something silly and everyone will laugh, breaking the tension. And when they leave for the day and Tom's on the veteran's bed,

they don't feel so bad."

Though the family of World War II army veteran Edwin Gehlert had seen how Tom had comforted him throughout his stay in hospice, it wasn't until they witnessed how the cat helped with their loved one's passing that they were thoroughly convinced of the contributions of the feline staffer.

The family gathered around the bed, aware that the end was near. Suddenly, Tom leapt onto the bed and curled up next to the man, and what he did next astonished everyone: The cat put his paw in Gehlert's hand, and after taking a couple more ragged breaths, the man died.

"I kept telling Daddy to let go, to go toward the light," said his daughter Pamela Thompson. "When Tom put his paw in Daddy's hand, it was like God was telling me he had ahold of my dad and that everything was okay."

"That cat took him right to heaven," said his wife, Elizabeth.

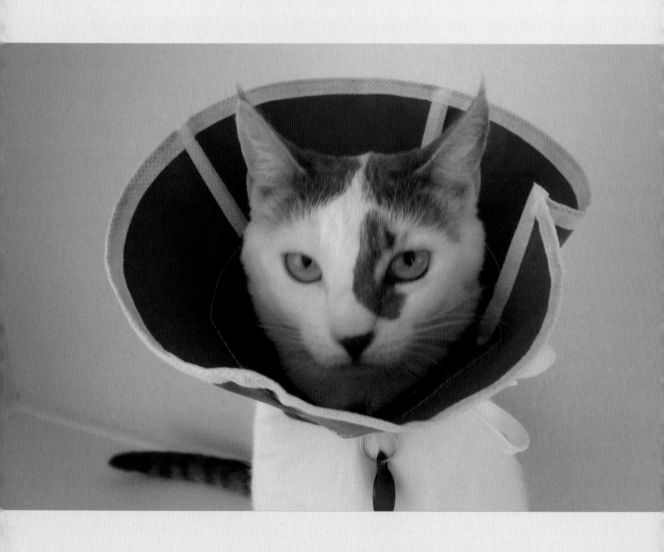

Teaching Assistant Cat

Arden Moore is a pet behavior consultant, author of twenty-four books about pets, and is a certified pet first-aid and CPR instructor often called upon to give presentations. She has found that the best way to demonstrate certain techniques is with a real live animal by her side. When she first started out, she'd watch some instructors use stuffed animals as models while others used their own calm, tolerant dogs to give students a more accurate hands-on experience.

No one offered presentations with a live cat, which isn't exactly a surprise. After all, how many cats would put up with the indignity of leaving home, traveling, and then being subjected to a variety of positions and wrapped in restraints and blankets — and the dreaded cone of shame — for hours, all in front of a group of complete strangers?

But Moore had recently nursed a rescued cat back to health, and through three months of intensive medical treatment, she had noticed that the cat — who she named Zeki — was exceptionally calm. Even her veterinarians commented

on the cat's easy-going demeanor.

So Moore started training Zeki in all of the hands-on techniques she taught in class. "She calmly accepted being wrapped in a towel, having her teeth brushed, her pulse taken, being fitted with a cat safety muzzle, having her nails clipped, and given a thorough head-to-tail examination," said Moore. "She seemed to be a natural teaching cat."

Zeki became known as the Pet Safety Cat and started to accompany Moore to serve as her teaching assistant at conferences and pet expos. They traveled together by plane and car to eight states and dozens of cities, and all the while Zeki never put up a fuss.

Indeed, Moore believed that the cat was absolutely born to help teach, which was superbly illustrated during a pet first-aid class they led at Camp-Run-A-Mutt in Point Loma, California. Moore was about to demonstrate how to perform chest compressions on a demo dog, when the students started laughing. When Moore looked up, they pointed at Zeki, who had jumped up onto the table in front of one of the stuffed demo dogs and started to knead the fake dog's chest as if she were performing dog CPR.

Unfortunately, Zeki passed away unexpectedly in the summer of 2014. Moore decided to continue her first-aid teaching legacy and has begun working with an orange tabby named Casey.

Pub Cat

Throughout Great Britain, you can find a pub on almost every corner, and over the centuries, many have named themselves after a cat or one of its body parts: the Cat's Eye Pub, the Cat's Whiskers, and the Cat and Fiddle are commonly found. As for an actual cat in a pub, well, they're pretty common, too. In fact, there's an online directory—PubCats.com—to help you locate resident felines in pubs all over the world.

In the United States, there are a number of pub-dwelling cats as well, and one of the best known is a gray-striped tabby by the name of Mr. Wu, who presides over Molly's at the Market, a family-run bar and restaurant located in the French Quarter of New Orleans. The cat first showed up at Molly's after Hurricane Katrina, and essentially never left.

Trey Monaghan, the human who works alongside Mr. Wu, said that his feline coworker has always pulled his weight, initially by helping out with crowd control. "When Wu first started to work with us, he was responsible for policing the bar of critters smaller than himself," he said. In addition to keeping the mice at bay, the

cat was also in charge of keeping dogs—the four-legged kind—out of the bar. But after a few years of such rugged work, Mr. Wu downshifted his responsibilities.

"Since working long nights in a French Quarter bar can age you quickly, Wu now spends half the days in the bar and the other half of the day in the office," said Monaghan. The cat's new responsibilities include reorganizing the office supplies, cleaning up after lunch, and using the adding machines to crunch numbers that he thinks are important.

Though there are stories about pub-dwelling felines who do occasionally imbibe in a nip or two from the taps, Mr. Wu has remained a teetotaler, hopping up onto a bar stool at least once a day to partake of his favorite, a shot glass of whipped cream.

Despite his worldwide following, Mon-

aghan said that Mr. Wu does his job like any other member of the family business, though he does get a little cantankerous early in the morning before breakfast. And just like at any business, there are occasional bumps and friction between employees. When Mr. Wu decides to grab a quick siesta, he doesn't like to be disturbed. And a few of the ladies in the office think he can be a little too aggressive when it comes to demanding head pats and scratches, as well as a convenient place to sleep.

"But for the most part, Wu knows his job," said Monaghan. "And he really does show up every day."

Music Studio Assistant Cat

Some people think cats are natural musicians, given their vocal range and ability to project, while more than a few musicians have relied on their feline companions for inspiration or just as a welcome break from the rigors of making and producing music.

Two separate cats have taken this process a step further, holding down important jobs steering musicians in the recording studio, helping to guide them through the challenge of producing and archiving music for all to hear.

At Vertigo Productions, a small recording studio and concert venue in Seattle, a silver tabby Exotic Shorthair cat named Winston is a multitalented feline employee that coworkers and visiting musicians and audience members appreciate.

Winston's official job title is studio assistant and community builder. "His job is to keep a mellow vibe in the studio, provide comic relief when things get tense, and offer up moral support through the creative process," said Jessica Kaminski, who runs the company with her husband, Brad. In a typical day,

Winston helps answer e-mails, oversees audio and video editing as well as poster design, and helps run Winston's Lair, the studio's acoustic concert series.

The cat can also soothe fragile egos and help temperamental musicians work through their disagreements. "Winston is particularly skilled at keeping morale high," Kaminski added, describing a recent late-night session where a few musicians were experiencing some creative differences. Just as the room was becoming tense, Winston sauntered in and plopped down, demanding attention and lightening the mood. "Hiring Winston was a no-brainer," said Kaminski. "His big personality, love of music, and ability to bring people together was a perfect fit for our studio."

Winston isn't the first cat to work in a recording studio. Back in 1988, musicians Dixie and Ed Eastridge were running Big Mo Studios in Kensington, Maryland, when they acquired a neighborhood cat named Kitty. They quickly realized that the cat appeared to wince whenever he heard the name. At the time, the majority of groups booking recording sessions at Big Mo were African American gospel groups. It was customary for the band members to call all of the white crew members Mike. So the Eastridges decided to rename the new feline Mike the Cat, and he moved in and promptly took over.

Mike the Cat started off by doing basic mouse security and plumping up the couch pillows for the musicians. With that experience under his belt, he moved on to the studio, where he spent a great deal of time sleeping on the soundboard in front of the playback speakers. "He seemed to find incredibly loud music very soothing," said Ed.

He also wasn't shy about speaking up, and among some musicians, Mike the Cat soon became known as the "Godfather of Meoyodeling." Jazz guitarist Danny Gatton took notice of the cat's skills when he was at Big Mo working with producer Dan Doyle on *New York Stories,* which was released by Blue Note Records. Toward the end of production, they were having trouble coming up with a name for one of the songs. Danny pointed at the studio's lone feline employee, who was sprawled out on the console, and said, "Call it 'Mike the Cat.'" And so they did. Dixie posed Mike the Cat at the piano for a photo, which appeared in the liner notes for the CD.

In 1992, Mike and his humans retired to Thetford, Vermont, where he traded his exciting life in the studio for one where he could live out his days in the mouse-filled barn of his dreams.

Actor Cat

As many cat people know, most cats aren't particularly eager to perform or do tricks, even if a treat is involved. So when animal trainer Rob Bloch set out in the fall of 1992 to train a cat to act in a supporting role on *Star Trek: The Next Generation,* he had his work cut out for him.

Working with his partner, Karen Thomas, Bloch, who runs the Critters of the Cinema acting talent agency, was assigned to provide a cat to play a feline character named Spot, owned by the character Lt. Commander Data, played by Brent Spiner. Another Spot had already appeared on the show, played by a different feline and trained by another team, but just as is the case with child or infant actors, most animals on TV and in film are played by multiple actors who look similar to each other but often have different strengths and talents.

At the time, Bloch had two buff orange cats named Brandy and Monster who had previously acted on several projects, and he immediately put them to work. "While dogs have more range, cats are trained to their own individual traits," he explained. "So when you train cats, you train them to do stuff that is

Geordi La Forge—played by LeVar Burton—were sitting at a table in Data's living quarters. The script called for Spot to jump onto the table and start to pester Data with a light swat or flick of the tail. Data set Spot back on the floor, only to have the cat jump back up. Monster played Spot in that scene, since he was the more active cat. In the second scene, later on in the movie, after the *Enterprise* had crashed and characters were frantically searching for survivors, Bloch placed Spot under some fake rubble so he could be found by the searchers. That scene required the cat to stay in one place, which meant it was Brandy's turn. Later on, Bloch added a third cat named Tyler to the roster in order to split work up between Monster and Brandy and allow them more time to rest, as well as giving the new cat time to adjust to being on a film set.

Just like human actors, feline stars occasionally clash with their fellow thespians. When Brandy first started working with Spiner, Bloch said the cat appeared to be bothered by Data's yellow eyes—which of course were contact lenses—perhaps because that iris color is extremely rare. Instead of paying attention to his trainers, Brandy stared at Spiner's eyes.

"Karen and I had to work a bit harder

within their personalities." Brandy excelled at lying around and was comfortable being held in an unfamiliar pair of arms without fighting or wiggling, while Monster was more of an action cat, so the pair switched back and forth as the scripts dictated.

For example, there were two cat scenes in the feature film *Star Trek: Generations*. In the first scene, Data and Lt. Commander

to keep his attention on the task at hand instead of Data's eyes," said Bloch, but after a day or two on the set, the cat relaxed and resumed his professional demeanor. "I doubt anyone, even the actor, noticed anything was different, but we trainers did."

While their *Star Trek* appearances were undoubtedly the cats' biggest role, they also appeared in a variety of commercials through the years, helped no doubt by their exposure on the popular TV show. Tyler acted in a Kodak commercial with Dennis Rodman in 1996, Monster crawled over a giant crayon for a Friskies commercial, and Brandy "slept" on an Oriental rug for a Cheez-It commercial.

Reiki Practitioner Cat

It's no secret that cats are well familiar with various alternative health practices. They've been long called Zen masters for their ability to sit still, and massage therapists for their ability to knead a certain spot for hours on end.

Gianna Settin, a Reiki practitioner who today lives in Colorado, lived in Bangor, Maine, in the 2000s with a black-and-white tuxedo cat named Willie. She had always thought he was unusual. For one, Willie liked to tag along when she hiked through the woods, constantly heeling by her side, and when he detected something unusual a little ways off, the cat would abruptly stop and go on point just like a bird dog. "I wasn't sure whether I had a dog or a cat," she joked.

When she first started learning Reiki, an ancient Japanese healing technique, she practiced on Willie: When she petted him, she practiced sending energy through her hand to his head. After a while, the cat seemed to ask for it, bumping his head against Settin's hand instead of just rubbing against her, as he did when he wanted to be petted.

She always knew Willie was a quick learner. Still, she was caught off guard when the cat began administering some Reiki of his own, sending along the treatment's trademark energy waves when he just happened to be sitting on a person's lap.

Settin often saw clients in her home office, and it was clear that Willie didn't want to be left out. When she opened the door to the treatment room at the end of a session, she'd often find Willie stretched out full length along the bottom of the door. "He wasn't sleeping," she said, "he was soaking up the Reiki. And it was difficult to persuade him to move out of the way."

Before long, he decided he wanted to work as her assistant. As a Reiki master teacher, Settin held regular workshops to train others in the practice, and despite a no-pets policy, Settin eventually allowed Willie into the room after receiving permission from students and clients. Willie would walk among the students during a class, and he'd usually zero in on a particular student, sit down next to them, and place a paw on their body. Often, the student would later tell Settin that Willie just happened to put his paw on a spot where they were having problems. Settin was heartened and believed that the cat wasn't looking for attention, but that he was drawn not only to receiving Reiki energy but to giving it as well.

Once she decided that no harm could come to him, Willie became an integral part of her treatment team, participating in sessions with those clients who requested his services and helping her to teach. During private sessions, he'd sit quietly in one spot staring at the client, and not budge: no self-grooming, sleeping, or moving around the room. And when the session was over, he left the room.

Therapy Cat

Cat lovers know that whenever they're hurting in some way—physically or emotionally—spending just a few minutes with a favorite feline can work wonders and even help speed their recovery.

It's no wonder that many medical professionals believe that pet therapy can be more valuable and effective than other forms of treatment. Even Florence Nightingale recommended the use of animal therapy for her patients. "A small pet is often an excellent companion for the sick, for long chronic cases especially," she wrote.

Though pets often work alongside a medical professional like a physical therapist or a social worker, an increasing number of cats are also making patients in hospitals, nursing homes, and other care facilities feel better just through their presence. Some even visit college campuses during exam weeks to help relieve students' stress.

Flash, a brown tabby cat who has lived with Jaetta Ferguson of Kokomo, Indiana, since 2008, became a certified therapy cat in 2012 at the age of four.

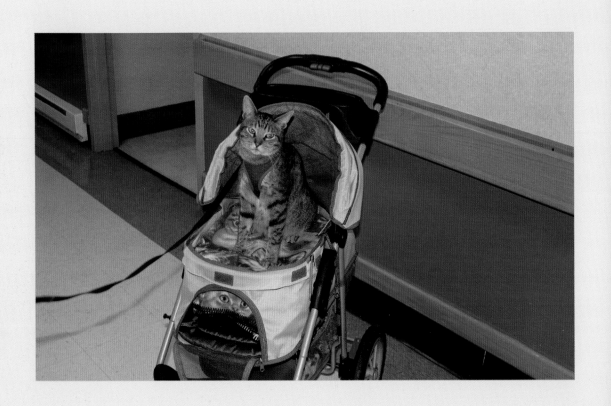

Together they visit people at local nursing homes and spend time at the public library to help kids improve their reading skills: A child reads aloud to him and Flash listens patiently and without judgment.

"He loves to socialize with people, so I knew I had to find something for us to do together," said Ferguson. They trained with a local chapter of Love on a Leash, a nationwide nonprofit organization that trains volunteers and their therapy pets. The pair regularly visits nine nursing homes in the area. They also attend several community events throughout the year, from parades and fairs to a costume contest and an Alzheimer's awareness walk.

There is a bit of work involved on the days when Flash conducts his therapy sessions. On visiting days, Ferguson gives Flash a sponge bath of sorts with baby wipes, his nails are clipped, and he's given a good brushing.

According to Ferguson, they don't visit just the residents in the nursing homes but also travel to spend time with the people who work there. "The staff loves when Flash visits them," she said. One time, they were visiting a patient who was petting Flash while a nurse looked on. Suddenly, the resident laughed for the first time since she moved into the home. "The nurse just about broke down crying because Flash brought so much love to this patient," said Ferguson. "That was pretty awesome to see."

Ferguson and Flash love their jobs so much that they even formed their own chapter of Love on a Leash to train more cat-and-human therapist pairs. "Basically, his job is to be cute and loving to people, which he does very well," said Ferguson. Of course, not every cat is cut out for the job, but for those who are, the rewards can be enormous for everyone involved.

Bodega Cat

Cats have a storied history of living in stores of all kinds to keep the rodent population at bay. Perhaps nowhere else have they become part of the landscape as much as in the small convenience and grocery stores of New York City, popularly known as bodegas.

Bodega cats call on a variety of skills when doing their jobs. Of course, most of their human coworkers will tell you that their primary job is to serve as chief mouse catcher, but their résumés have expanded to include a diverse array of skills. Some serve as greeters, akin to the Walmart type, though if they don't feel like it, they simply ignore you. Others believe that their job is to curl up and sleep in impossible places or next to packages and boxes that throw a bright spotlight onto their cuteness. Still other bodega cats will accompany customers on their rounds up and down the aisles to occasionally point out products that were not on their original shopping lists.

"A New York City bodega cat needs to be both amiable and fearless, having chosen a life that involves smiling while working the retail side of the

gig and also fending off unsavory characters and critters," said Phillip Mlynar, a journalist based in Brooklyn who has written about bodega cats and is partial to a small ginger cat at a nearby store who hides among a plastic flower display while surveying the scene. "I think there's something homey about entering a run-down store lit with lurid lighting and being greeted by a cat. Plus, I think we all like to secretly believe the cats are running the entire show."

While the prime occupational hazard of a bodega cat is a surprise visit from the health inspector—technically, it's illegal in New York City to have an animal of any kind in close proximity to where food is being served, even wrapped in plastic—occasionally a customer can't resist the cuteness and the desire to bring them home.

Even celebrities are unable to fight their siren call. Debbie Harry admitted that she once got a calico cat from a corner store. "I got her at a bodega," she said. "She was a tiny kitten and she was covered with fleas. I thought she was adorable so I took her home."

On the whole, bodega cats hold sway over their human counterparts, designing their own schedules despite what their two-legged coworkers may think. "Most store owners seem to ignore the cats most of the time, other than feeding them," said Mlynar. "Micromanagement is definitely not part of the bodega cat deal."

Urszula Jawor, who runs a small grocery in Williamsburg, Brooklyn, concurs. "In the morning she is lazy, it is her nap time," she said of her feline employee, a gray long-haired cat named Halloween. "But in the afternoon she is busy. She spends hours stalking the mice and the rats."

In Greenpoint, Brooklyn, bodega owner Andre Duran had nothing but praise for his tuxedo-clad four-legged employee named Oreo. "No one's ever complained about cat hair in their sandwiches, and if she weren't here, you bet there'd be bigger problems than hair."

Foster Parent Cat

One day in Norfolk, Great Britain, in 2007, a cat named Sky gave birth to four kittens. Sky's human was an animal lover named David Page, who loved the petite tortoiseshell cat. Page checked in on the mother cat and kittens several times a day to make sure everything was okay. He marveled at how quickly she embraced her job as new mother, and the kittens thrived.

A couple of days later, a Rottweiler named Roxy also gave birth to six puppies on some property Page owned nearby. But unlike Sky, who had happily embraced motherhood, unfortunately Roxy refused to nurse the puppies. Page believed that Roxy became stressed by the birth — as some new mothers do, both human and animal — and so he scooped up the puppies and brought them to his local veterinarian, who examined them and started them on a round of antibiotics.

Sadly, by the time Page had discovered them, the puppies were in pretty bad shape, and two of them had already succumbed to pneumonia. Page was understandably distraught and wanted to help the remaining pups. He decided

the only thing to do was to see if his cat Sky would pitch in.

"I put the four that were still alive at that stage in her box very gently one by one alongside her kittens just to see what happened," he said. "They snuggled into her straightaway."

But then they started doing more than snuggling up to Sky for warmth: They actually started nursing, which the mother cat not only accepted but encouraged wholeheartedly.

"It's not unusual for animals to be nurturing toward any species," said John C. Wright, Ph.D., coauthor of *Ain't Misbehavin': The Groundbreaking Program for Happy, Well-Behaved Pets and Their People,* and a certified applied animal behaviorist and professor of psychology at Mercer University. "The instinct to care for another animal can be hormonal or simply related to age. If they're young, their behavior is malleable, and they're open to just about any experience, opportunity, or companion. Like humans, animals, for the most part, yearn for company."

"It's just amazing to think that Sky has taken so well to the puppies," said Page. "She has a lovely, gentle nature and treats them just like her kittens. They are one big happy family."

And while for some felines, foster parenting is a one-time freelance job, others turn to it again and again, eager to get to work when a needy youngster arrives.

Church Cat

Cats have long lived in churches, particularly in the United Kingdom. Whether they're formally adopted by the church or live as mostly feral churchyard cats, there are reams of illuminated medieval manuscripts that chronicle churches' resident felines and that have small illustrations of cats roaming across the borders as a monk or two looks on benevolently.

During her November 2013 visit to Southwark Cathedral in London, Queen Elizabeth paid homage to Doorkins Magnificat, the church's resident brown tabby, with a couple of scratches on the head as he snoozed away in the bishop's chair in the sanctuary, totally oblivious to the royal presence that surrounded him.

Today, perhaps the most well-known church cat in Great Britain is Louis, an orange tabby who lives at Wells Cathedral in Somerset, in England's southwest corner. He likes to stick to his own company most of the time, lounging on the grass outside the massive twelfth-century building in warm weather and next to a radiator in the northern nave in wintertime. But he has been known

to bring a smile to the face of the bishop and parishioners alike on the occasions when he's decided to take a casual stroll up the aisle right in the middle of a service.

Louis first showed up in 2005 as a stray, and it didn't take long before he thoroughly ingratiated himself into daily life at the cathedral, which has a small gift shop where visitors can purchase a variety of items with Louis's face on it, from key chains to mugs. One of the parishioners even wrote a children's book about him, and it's possible that a good number of visitors to the cathedral have absolutely no interest in learning about the history of the church: They just want to catch a glimpse of Louis. Fans who can't make the trek to visit him in person can send messages to him via his Louis Cathcat Facebook page.

As is often the case, word travels quickly among the local feline population when it comes to a place to stay with a cushy job and plenty to eat, and Lindsay Mann, a staffer at Wells, has reported that Louis's tenure as sole church cat may be ending. "Louis is in danger of having competition as the only cat in the cathedral," said Mann. A local cat named Pangur, who lives at the Black Dog Pottery shop nearby, has decided that he likes to hang out at the cathedral. "While Louis and Pangur aren't the best of friends, they do tolerate each other's presence with a certain aloofness," she added.

Perhaps Pangur too will have a children's book in his future.

Train Stationmaster Cat

An eviction notice doesn't typically result in a happy ending, let alone good employment prospects for the future, for either humans or cats. But when a small regional train company in western Japan decided to take unusual action, they not only avoided bankruptcy but also gave a new lease on life to a soon-to-be-homeless cat.

In 2006, the Wakayama Electric Railway in Kinokawa was losing almost five million dollars a year, and though they had cut down to a barebones schedule, the trains that did operate were running mostly empty. Meanwhile, a small grocery near the railway's Kishigawa station was slated for demolition, and a stray calico cat who hung around the store was going to become homeless as a result. Despite his business troubles and the fact that he preferred dogs, railway president Mitsunobu Kojima offered to see what he could do, though he offered no promises.

But when he met Tama, everything changed.

"The moment I met eyes with Tama, I was immediately struck with an image of Tama as stationmaster," Kojima said. Suddenly, he realized that the cat could save his rail company from ruin. In his eyes, Tama was a *maneki neko,* a real-life example of the ubiquitous ceramic Japanese cats that people believe attract both luck and money, found at the entrances to homes and businesses all over the country and the world.

On January 5, 2007, Tama was officially installed as stationmaster, wearing a cap made from following the same pattern as the full-size caps that her coworkers wore, though Kojima said it wasn't easy to customize the cap to fit Tama's small head. Ultimately, it took three seamstresses to finish up the job.

Once Tama settled in, word quickly spread about the feline stationmaster, and soon people were traveling from all over the country to visit the cat, who worked from her office in a ticket booth. Ridership increased by 10 percent the first year, and people who had traveled long distances wanted to take home a souvenir of their trip, which led to a gift shop in the station where fans could purchase books about Tama, mugs and T-shirts with her picture on them, and even a cat-themed dinette set. Kojima then designed a special Tama train, with cat-shaped seats and a cartoon version of the feline stationmaster prancing around on the outside of the train, leaving a trail of pawprints behind.

Not only was the rail line saved, but Kojima estimated that Tama generated almost eleven million dollars for the rail line and the town during her first full year of employment. In 2008, Kojima rewarded the hardworking feline stationmaster with a promotion; her new title became Super Stationmaster and her fame grew. She even starred in a Japanese TV commercial for Aflac, costarring with the waddling duck mascot.

As tens of thousands of tourists flocked to see Tama each year, Kojima decided to upgrade the station in 2010, redesigning the exterior to resemble a cat's face. Tama received another promotion to become Operating Officer, making her the first feline — and first female — to become an executive of a railroad corporation. In 2013, she was named Deputy President of the rail line.

Despite her many promotions, Tama's main job has remained pretty much the same: to welcome visitors and look cute. But with thousands of fans who show up each month, Tama is never really off the clock. "She never complains, even though passengers touch her all over the place," said railway spokeswoman Yoshiko Yamaki. "She's an amazing cat. She has patience and charisma; she's the perfect stationmaster."

Mayor Cat

In a political climate where many people would like to clean house and just "throw the bums out" and start fresh, I'd venture to guess that more than a few would be willing to let a feline take the reins for a while.

The truth is that cats — and other animals — have campaigned in a variety of political elections through the years, but only a small percentage have won. One of those winning candidates is an orange tabby named Stubbs, who has served as mayor of Talkeetna, Alaska — population 876 — since 1997, a longer tenure than many two-legged mayors. Rumor has it that he was elected as a write-in candidate when locals were fed up with that year's roster of possibilities, but a few locals later admitted that Stubbs was informally appointed to the honorary position, since Talkeetna's governing board is a community council. Those folks didn't mind sharing a bit of the power, and neither did Stubbs.

Named for his tailless state when plucked from a box of free kittens in front of Nagley's General Store, Stubbs soon took up residence inside the store, where his constituents could find him to air any grievances and complaints. The

store is next to the West Rib Café & Pub, where Stubbs has been known to imbibe his favorite drink—a wineglass filled with water and liberally spiked with catnip—even in broad daylight. In a state where winters are long and dark, most people tend to look the other way.

There are no real job responsibilities since the position of mayor is largely symbolic in the small village, but most residents take it in stride. Stubbs doesn't do much, but they know that neither would most human elected or appointed officials.

For their part, his constituents approve of the job he's done. "He hasn't voted for anything I wouldn't have voted for," said resident Peg Vos.

Gil Gunther, who runs the Antler Outpost gift shop, concurred. "Anything's better than a human," he said.

The mayor's major accomplishment has been attracting tourists to the town, once news began to spread about his position. But after being interviewed by CNN, *The Wall Street Journal,* and countless other media outlets from around the world, success still hasn't gone to his head.

The cat does borrow a page from many two-legged political figures, making the rounds of the various restaurants and shops in town to keep tabs on his constituents' concerns and suggestions. He also openly and unashamedly accepts bribes of stray bits of salmon and king crab.

But in this small town in the shadow of Mount McKinley, no one seems to mind.

Composer Cat

Creativity can strike anywhere, even in the brain of a cat.

Ketzel was a black-and-white tuxedo cat living happily in New York City with her humans when in the mid-1990s the urge to compose a piece of music suddenly overtook her. Within a few short months, her burst of creativity resulted in an award-winning short piano piece that went on to earn her fame and even a few royalty checks.

It all happened one morning in 1996, when one of her human companions, Morris Moshe Cotel, chairman of the composition department at the renowned Peabody Conservatory, was getting ready to work. Professor Cotel was working from home that day, and he liked to play a Bach prelude and fugue on the piano as a warm-up exercise. Ketzel, three years old at the time, had long been partial to Bach, and after Cotel finished playing, the cat leapt onto the piano bench as inspiration struck.

"She put one paw down and very slowly walked down the keyboard, as if she were stalking an invisible mouse," said Cotel.

Her creativity was contagious. Cotel was impressed by what he'd heard, and quickly transcribed the notes Ketzel played as she made her way from the right side of the keyboard—where the highest notes are—down to the left, heavy with low gut bass tones.

"He said, 'This piece has a beginning, a middle, and an end. How can this be? It's written by a cat,'" his wife, Aliya Cheskis-Cotel, later remarked, adding that her husband was particularly struck by the "structural elegance" of the composition.

After he finished transcribing the piece—which was less than a minute in length—Cotel forgot about it. A few months later, he heard about a composition contest that requested works that lasted sixty seconds or less. None of his own compositions fit the bill, but Ketzel's piece did. So he typed it up without any changes, called it "Piece for Piano, Four Paws," listed Ketzel Cotel as the composer, and sent it off to the contest.

To his surprise, about a month later, he received a letter from the contest judges: they awarded the piece a special mention. "We gave the piece serious consideration because it was quite well written," said Guy Livingston, who helped wade through the entries. "It reminded us of Anton Webern, and if Webern had a cat, this is what Webern's cat would have written."

From that point on, Ketzel was on the fast track. "Piece for Piano, Four Paws" had its world premiere at the Peabody in 1998 and was subsequently performed live throughout Europe. Royalty checks started to show up; the first was for $19.72 and of course was written out to Ketzel Cotel.

"We thought, how are we going to cash this?" said Cheskis-Cotel. "Luckily, at the bank, they knew my husband, and they allowed us to cash it."

Ketzel's piece went on to appear on a CD entitled *Purrfectly Classical,* a compilation of cat-themed music, and she was profiled in the 2007 book *The World of Women in Classical Music.*

When the piece was slated to be performed at a concert at the Museum of the City of New York and Cheskis-Cotel informed the promoters that the composer planned to attend the concert, they were dubious. Only when Cheskis-Cotel informed them that the feline composer was already wearing her tuxedo did they consent.

When the pianist performing the piece — second-to-last on the program — announced, "Ladies and gentlemen, the next piece, believe it or not, was written by Ketzel the Cat," Ketzel meowed loudly to acknowledge her name. Cheskis-Cotel then flipped open Ketzel's carrier, lifted her up, and ran to the front of the audience.

Ketzel took three bows, and the audience applauded wildly.

Stable Cat

Some cats seek out jobs for themselves.

These self-sufficient felines don't need a human to give them a job, but take the initiative to go out and find one on their own. Once they secure a place of employment, they pretty much run their own show; in a way, they're consummate feline freelancers and entrepreneurs.

Setting up shop at a horse stable is a smart choice, given that grain and feed tends to attract mice and other rural rodents. Perhaps most important, the resident humans are happy to have these cat colleagues, regardless of how they make their way onto the payroll.

Mill Ridge Farm in Lexington, Kentucky, is home to a number of stable cats—at least one per barn—and their human coworkers basically allow them free rein. Contrary to tales of barn cats being unfriendly and scared of people, a black cat named Princess has been charming both humans and horses since she first showed up at the farm.

Though the most important skill a cat can possess is to be a superb mouser,

Princess has talents in other areas as well. "Mousing is her job, and she does it very well," said Kim Poulin, assistant sales manager at the farm. But in between her patrolling duties, whenever Princess spots a person or horse, she makes a beeline to rub up against them in exchange for a few pats or nuzzles in return.

"She thinks that she runs the barn that she lives in," Poulin added, which naturally extends to any vehicles that might be in the vicinity. As a result, staff and visitors are regularly warned to roll up the windows of their cars and trucks or else Princess will hop right in to conduct a thorough inspection before spending her coffee break on a pleasure drive around the premises.

Babysitter Cat

Finally, the youngest feline worker in the entire book.

Since the general rule of thumb is that cats age seven years for each of our human years, it's actually no surprise that cats sometimes step up to the plate and start their careers far sooner than we'd expect.

But a kitten named Chesney caught everyone off guard when in the summer of 2012 he started his first job at the tender age of only eight weeks. The orange kitten was living at the Exeter Axhayes Adoption Centre in Devon, England, at the time. As is the case at most animal shelters and rescue facilities, human staffers can expect a steady stream of new residents all months of the year, but it becomes especially heavy in the summertime.

Chesney had settled in with his mother and two siblings when a two-week-old kitten was brought to the shelter after a worker found him abandoned by the side of the road. His mother had been struck by a car while she was crossing the street. In such cases, shelter employees move quickly to merge or-phaned kittens in with another litter so that they can get the warmth and nour-

ishment they need in order to survive. This kitten — the staff had named him Joey — nestled
in with Chesney's mom alongside her three
kittens.

Happily, the mother cat and all her kittens quickly accepted Joey. However, he was
singled out by Chesney, who decided to take
Joey under his wing, helping the younger
kitten while also taking some of the parenting pressure off Chesney's mom. Soon,
Chesney was acting as chief babysitter for
Joey, who clearly enjoyed his jaunts outside
with his older, more experienced caretaker.

It just goes to show that some cats just
want a job to do, no matter how old — or
young — they are.

Notes

INTRODUCTION

3. *he simply refused to take action* Oswell Blakeston, *Working Cats*. (London: Elek Books, 1963), 22.

3. *a contract for his services* Ibid, 11.

3. *fulfilling certain specialized duties* Ibid.

MESSENGER CAT

20. *back are scratch-free* Sara Malm, "Postman Pet: Courier Cycles up to 25 Miles with His CAT on His Shoulder While Making Deliveries," *Daily Mail* (London), November 8, 2012, http://www.dailymail.com.uk/news/article-2229834/Real-life-Postman-pat-Courier-delivers-parcels-cat-companion.html

20. *she arrived via bicycle* Ibid.

20. *about taking her out* "Former NJ Man Has Cat for Co-Pilot When He Rides Bicycle Around Philadelphia," *Newark Star-Ledger*, May 23, 2013.

ROOMMATE CAT

26. *for a long time* Mie Sakamoto, "Things Look Up for Tokyo's Jilted Felines," *Japan Times*, March 26, 2014.

SERVICE CAT

32. *to stay by Lorcan's side* Amanda Cable,

"The Seven-Year-Old Boy Trapped in a Silent World," *Daily Mail* (London), September 12, 2012.

32. *like winning all over again* Ibid.

EXERCISE TRAINER CAT

37. *the more she purred* Ira Dreyfuss, "Lifting Cats, Babies Now a Form of Exercise," *Vancouver Columbian*, October 28, 1997.

38. *go for it* Bob Ivry, "Cats, Beware: You're the Latest Fitness Gadget," *Bergen County Record*, November 14, 1997.

38. *listening to her to stop* Ibid.

DIABETIC ALERT CAT

56. *and raises the alarm* Jamie Bullen, "Whitstable Family Claims Sixth Sense of RSPCA Rescue Cat Pippa Saved Diabetic Daughter's Life," *Kent Online*, March 25, 2014, http://www.kentonline.co.uk/canterbury/news/abandoned-cat-proves-to-be-14689.

56. *sleep a little easier at night* Ibid.

MILITARY WORKING CAT

61. *our mobility rodent deterrent* Air-man 1st Class Mike Young, "Supply Group Uses 'Military Working Cat' to Control Critters," *US Federal News Service,* July 30, 2007, www.edwards.af.mil/news/story.asp?id=123062496.

THEATER CAT

73. *they can upstage the actors* Louise Jury, "Theatre Director Has Kittens Over Tiffany's Felines," *The Standard* (London), September 23, 2009.

CAT BURGLAR CAT

81. *two or three things back each day* "Underwear Thief Is Real Cat Burglar," REX USA, *Solent News,* July 8, 2010.

WRITER'S MUSE CAT

104. *I find that kind of nice* Lisa Angowski Rogak, *The Cat on My Shoulder: Writers and Their Cats* (Stamford, CT: *Longmeadow Press,* 1993), 59.

104. *from a deadly pervasive ignorance* William S. Burroughs, *The Cat Inside* (New York: Penguin Books, 2002), 46.

MODEL CAT

106. *feel better about wearing the clothes* Tomo Kosuga, "Puss in Boots," *Vice.com,* April 1, 2008, http://www.vice.com/read/puss-in-boots-v15n4.

ARTIST CAT

117. *they just wander off* Alice Coote, "A Paw Print? It's An Original," *Herald Sun* (Melbourne), February 6, 2012.

HOSPICE CAT

133. *first day he was here* Tom Cramer, "Tabby Cat Makes Life Easier for Dying Veterans," Veterans Health Administration, November 6, 2014.

133. *they don't feel so bad* Ibid.

133. *everything was okay* Ibid.

133. *That cat took him right to heaven* Ibid.

BODEGA CAT

161. *so I took her home* Emma Rosenblum, "Party Lines," *New York*, October 16, 2006.

161. *stalking the mice and the rats* Kate Hammer, "To Dismay of Inspectors, Prowling Cats Keep Rodents on the Run at City Delis," *New York Times*, December 21, 2007.

161. *bigger problems than hair* Ibid.

FOSTER PARENT CAT

165. *I put the four* "Cat Adopts Rottweiler Puppies," *Mumbai Mirror*, July 9, 2007.

165. *It's not unusual for animals* Alice Cooke, "Extraordinary Animal Friendships," *Country Life* (UK), January 18, 2011.

165. *It's just amazing* "Rottweiler Pup Whose Mum's a Moggy," *Daily Mail* (London), July 6, 2007.

TRAIN STATIONMASTER CAT

171. *Tama as stationmaster* Johnny Strategy, "Tama — The Station Master Cat Who Raised Over $10 Million and Helped Save a Train Line," *Spoon & Tamago*, August 13, 2013, http://www.spoon-tamago.com/2013/08/13/tama-the-station-master-cat.

172. *she's the perfect stationmaster* "Cat Oversees Japanese Train Station, Brings Back Passengers," *USA Today*, May 26, 2008.

MAYOR CAT

175. *I wouldn't have voted for* Jim Carlton, "Mayor of Alaskan Town Is a Cat," *Wall Street Journal*, October 15, 2013.

175. *Anything's better than a human* Ibid.

COMPOSER CAT

177. *stalking an invisible mouse* Aaron Levin, "Piano Cat," *The Johns Hopkins Gazette Online*, January 20, 1998, http://pages.jh.edi/-gazette/janmar98/jan2098/20piano.html.

178. *It's written by a cat* James Barron, "Noted Composer, Who Leapt Into Atonality, Meows Her Last," *New York Times*, July 18, 2011.

178. *Webern's cat would have written* Ibid.

179. *allowed us to cash it* Ibid.

Photo Credits

Crossing Guard Cat: Monti Franckowiak

Farmer Cat: Ken & Greta Cook

Bookstore Cat: Boswell close-up, and with *New Yorker* book: Nancy Eisenstein; Boswell on shelf: Maria Uprichard

Office Cat: Catastrophe: Chantal Roberts; Pawprints in concrete: Scott Gorley; London: Melissa Nelson

Messenger Cat: Adam Harnett/Caters News Agency

Dog Trainer Cat: Cheeto in Tree: Kat Albrecht/MissingPetPartnership.org; Cheeto on grass with dog: Susan Tiftick

Roommate Cat: Tokyo Cat Guardian

Firehouse Cat: Jessica Mikel-Bertolini

Service Cat: Copyright © Jayne Dillon 2013

Boat Captain Cat: Capt. Chris Perunko

Exercise Trainer Cat: REX USA/Mike Hollist/Daily Mail/Rex

Nurse Cat: Popeye lying down: Cassidee Goodnight; Popeye portrait: Lise Greil Photography

Circus Cat: Amazing Acro-Cats/Samantha Martin; Nine cats with Samantha Martin: Steve Grubman

Security Guard Cat: REX USA/Rosie Hallam/Rex

Minister Cat: REX USA/Martin McCullough

Diabetic Alert Cat: Lauren Campbell/
Caters News Agency

Celebrity Cat: REX USA/MediaPunch
Inc.; in limo: REX USA/Dan Callister/
Rex

Military Working Cat: Airman 1st Class
Mike Young/United States Air Force

Navy Cat: Simon: PDSA; cat with
Winston Churchill, and cat in gunwale:
Australian War Memorial; Tiddles, cat
with rope: Lt. C.H. Parnall, Royal Navy
Official Photographer

Fast-Food Employee Cat: Pizza Hut Japan

Theater Cat: Orange and white cat: REX
USA/Photo by Alex Lentati / Evening
Standard/Rex; Tuxedo cat: REX USA /
Rex

Library Cat: Jan Louch

Cat Burglar Cat: Dusty: Jean Chu; Lingerie
Cat: REX USA/Solent News/Rex

Police Cat: Miyazu Police Station of Kyoto
Prefectural Police

Distillery Cat: Maker's Mark Distillery Inc.

Cat Café Cat: Fluffs/cat with cup: REX
USA/www.maverickartsclub.com/Rex;
people with cats and cups: REX USA/
Stuart Clarke/Rex

News Anchor Cat: TV Tokyo Corporation

Musician Cat: Musashi: REX USA; Nora
the Piano Cat: Burnell Yow! and Betsy
Alexander

Writer's Muse Cat: Eleanor Garvey

Model Cat: Nesta in lion hat: Yumiko Landers / Nesta's Nest; All others: Copyright © Artisan Crew/cushzilla
.com — Photos for Leah Workman

Furniture Tester Cat: CatastrophiCreations

Artist Cat: REX USA / Newspix / Rex

Hotel Concierge Cat: Peter Loppacher

Weather Observer Cat: Courtesy of Mount

Washington Observatory
Tour Guide Cat: Jalan.com
Hospice Cat: Tom portrait: Marian Mc-
   Connell; Tom with Erwin "Skip"
   Wyman: Laura Hart / Salem VA
Teaching Assistant Cat: Arden Moore
Pub Cat: Marianna Massey / Licensed by
   James Monaghan III
Music Studio Assistant Cat: Winston: jek-
   aminski/Vertigo Productions; Mike the
   Cat: John Sprung
Actor Cat: Dennis Rodman with Tyler:
   Rob Bloch / Critters of the Cinema;
   Star Trek / Brent Spiner: REX USA;
   Brandy: Rob Bloch / Critters of
   the Cinema
Reiki Practitioner Cat: Copyright ©
   Gianna Settin 2006
Therapy Cat: Jaetta Ferguson

Bodega Cat: Phillip Mlynar
Foster Parent Cat: REX USA/Jerry Daws
Church Cat: in church: REX USA/London
   News Pictures/Rex; with Queen: REX
   USA/Paul Grover/Rex
Train Stationmaster Cat: Getty Images/
   Toru Yamanaka
Mayor Cat: Lauri Stec
Composer Cat: Sivan Cotel
Stable Cat: Courtesy of Mill Ridge Farm
Babysitter Cat: REX USA/Richard Aus-
   tin/Rex

Acknowledgments

For supplying me with details and photos of their own cats on the job, thanks go to Monti Franckowiak, Ken and Greta Cook, Nancy Eisenstein, Chantal Roberts, Kat Albrecht, Yoko Yamamoto, Jessica Mikel and the firefighters of Engine 22 Ladder 13 in Manhattan, Jess Barratt, Captain Christopher Perunko, Kristin Conrad, Samantha Martin, Gill Hubbard, Yuko Koki, Jan Louch, Jean Chu and Jim Coleman, Nori Akashi, Jacklyn Evans and Sydina Bradshaw, Kyoko Komatsuzawa, Burnell Yow! and Betsy Alexander, Ken Morton, David Laing, Yumiko Landers, Leah Workman and Hiroshi Hibino, Mike Wilson and Megan Hanneman, Louise Clayton and Tegan Ellis, Nicholas Sciammarella, Krissy Fraser and Mike Carmon, Marian McConnell, Laura Hart and Dorothy Rizzo, Arden Moore, Trey Monaghan, Jessica Kaminski, Ed and Dixie Eastridge, Rob Bloch, Gianna Settin, Jaetta Ferguson, Phillip Mlynar, Lindsay Mann, Lauri Stec, Aliya Cheskis-Cotel, Kim Poulin, Laura Watts, and Dan Thomas.

Eternal thanks be to Superagent, aka Scott Mendel.

Thanks also to Peter Joseph at Thomas Dunne Books/St. Martins Press, as well as Tom Dunne, Sally Richardson, and the late Matthew Shear, for launching this whole critter trajectory starting with *The Dogs of War*, followed by *Dogs of Courage,* and then on to *One Big Happy Family.* Thanks also to Laura Clark, Melanie Fried, Staci Burt, Kathryn Hough, Kelsey Lawrence, Christy D'Agostini, and Joan Higgins, for helping make all of my books shine.

And to Alex Ishii, for being my best first reader.